NOIR

Olivier Pauvert is a pharmacist in
a small town in south-west France.
He is 34 years old. *Noir* is his first novel.

Adriana Hunter has translated nearly
thirty books including works by Agnès
Desarthe, Amélie Nothomb, Frédéric
Beigbeder and Catherine Millet, and has
been shortlisted for the *Independent* Foreign
Fiction Prize twice. She lives in Norfolk
with her husband and their three children.

D1262489

NOIR

Olivier Pauvert

translated by Adriana Hunter

COUNTERPOINT
BERKELEY

Library of Congress Cataloging-in-Publication Data

Pauvert, Olivier.
[Noir. English]
Noir / Olivier Pauvert ; translated by Adriana Hunter.
p. cm.
ISBN-13: 978-1-58243-447-6
ISBN-10: 1-58243-447-6
I. Hunter, Adriana. II. Title.

PQ2716.A382N613 2007
843'.92—dc22

2008013101

Printed in the United States of America

Counterpoint
2117 Fourth Street
Suite D
Berkeley, CA 94710
www.counterpointpress.com

Distributed by Publishers Group West

10 9 8 7 6 5 4 3 2 1

To Japanese coffee mills

I

I AM JUST TAKING A LONG DRAG on the joint when I hear the sound. Surprised, we turn towards the bank where the noise is coming from. After a few seconds of silence there is a gurgling, a moist sigh. The other man looks at me and I know what he is thinking: behind this mound a couple of jokers are making the most of the cool grass and the deep dark night to fuck. I put down my empty glass, snigger and pass him the stub to free up my hands. We climb the little rise on our hands and knees. There is indeed a Venus there, below us. Naked. She is hanging from the tree by a wire, and her feet are swinging ten centimetres above the black earth. Black with blood. The body has been ripped open and her entrails hang down over her legs. She gives off the most unbearable smell, the stench of human insides, the stink of flesh.

I know that smell, I discovered it during a brief spell in intensive care, the net result of a car chase while under the influence. Because it was a second offence, I picked up six months' community service, which, according to his lordship the Judge, would turn me back into a responsible citizen. Six months emptying bedpans in the antechamber to the great hereafter, that boudoir where people – plugged in and wired up like a space shuttle about to take off – wait for the end of the countdown that will launch them towards Saint Peter (or Paul or James, they are not too fussy by then). A young doctor from Luxembourg suggested I should go and watch the autopsy of some poor man who had choked to death on his liquidised food. That was my first rendezvous with dead flesh and its smell. No chance of a gradual acquaintance, oh no: this was the full works. Death from the outside, death from the inside, and even from the space in between.

This girl is definitely dead, no doubt about that. The steel wire has sliced her neck right through to the bone. Her right eye has been gouged out. I stay where I am, watching her swaying. I can't feel my body any more. The other guy stands there throwing up, then sinks to his knees and throws up again, and then again on all fours, coughing, until his stomach can only produce painful spasms, which connect him to the ground by a thread of yellowish bile. For a moment I feel nothing: mind and body are reduced to stone. Silence settles. Everything freezes. In the distance I can see each individual street light in the town. On that tree I know every branch, and on each branch every leaf, consumed in slow motion by countless caterpillars. On that body I can see each wound, each blow, the warped shape of the broken skull. I can feel the heat of the corpse evaporating into the air like a swirling cloud of moths.

I recognise this girl. She's the girl from the bar, the one who was barefoot.

Later, I am sitting on the grass. Up above, dawn streaks the sky with its bevies of pink clouds. A man beside me is doing everything he can to bring me back to reality. I don't know how long I have been sitting here like a statue, looking at the tree with its strange fruit, my whole mind diluted in that image.

The eighteenth hole won't be passable for a while. It looks like a multicoloured car park of red, blue and white vehicles, dotted with flashing lights, revolving silently. They've carved deep ruts in the beautiful carpet of grass, while ribbons of fluorescent light weave an extraordinary criss-cross of mysterious, shifting zones. As I get back up and vaguely stammer my identity, it strikes me that I am at the centre of the innermost circle, the one on whom everything converges. The circle of the tree and of the girl.

I'm searched, handcuffed and taken away. This will be my second trip in a police van, and under different circumstances I might have found it affecting. I can remember the sense of glory, of triumph, when I managed to be nabbed by the police when I was still a minor. The motive: playing pinball when I was underage. Some zealous officer of the law saw fit to haul my acne all the way to the station, reckoning it would make up a full set with the chancres and the giant carbuncles. During the night my grandfather, old man Stroppinni, came to get me; a proud upright figure among the junkies and the drunks. The acne went. The story lingered.

I get in. The little police van has enough smells in it for a huge station. It is as if the worn metal has been impregnated with the odours of every arse that has ever sat down here. It oozes with old tramp, prostitute crud and police sweat. They sit the other man down opposite me: glassy eyed and green faced, he looks out at the dawn through the mesh on the window. Two vast stalagmites of meat in police uniforms keep an eye on us, just in case, just in case something happens. They can be sure of one thing: nothing will happen. We stay there meekly handcuffed to those two lumps. The van sets off, hurtling through the countryside to the north of Nice under a candy-pink sky. I try to think, to remember how it all started. The wedding, the club, the little ripples on the lake, a lovely evening barely disrupted by gastronomic and sartorial excess, the puking fits and the squealing laughter of various guests: each to his own, Bacchus to all. I think of my wife, my children. I am clutched by anxiety, gripped by a searing kiss of fear.

'Where are we going?' I say.

The officer sitting to my right lifts his chin and brings his gaze down on me.

'Be quiet,' he replies with a contemptuous smirk, his voice deep, almost hoarse.

'I'd like to make a phone call. Where are we going?'

He looks at me again and in his hooded, whiskery eyes I can see the flicker of his conquerors. Not the sort who conquered Everest, oh no: the conquerors in the elections. They promised order, a vigorous militia and an effective judicial system, and the people cheered and cried 'More! More! Go for it!' as the electoral orgasm drew near. After that day-long clinch in the narrow confines of the polling booth a new kind of government was born, a multi-headed hydra of charismatic leaders. Of course there were a few who challenged the legitimacy of this new order, who questioned

4

the purity of the publicised intentions, the need for the purges, the salubriousness of the camps. But the riots were quelled calmly and with all due respect to the rights of the individual, apparently, and in the autumn everything did, in fact, settle down. The challenges dropped away like the leaves from the trees. One leaf at a time on those calm mornings when fists hammered on doors, or in whole spinneys on the days when there were major round-ups. After that we grew accustomed to an icy silence as winter settled.

Having had a really good look at me, he smiles slyly at his colleague, then ruffles my hair in an almost affectionate gesture.

'Who would you call, hmm? How can you hope to change anything now? Things have to happen the way they're meant to.' After a pause he carries on. 'You've done a good job, but your time's up.'

The van bounces along from one pothole to the next. Every bend is negotiated at breakneck speed, slewing me from right to left along the scraggy metal bench on which I am now resigned to leaving my own smell. My nose is bleeding and so are my ears. The other man looks at me for a moment, then closes his eyes. I can see his chest rising feebly from time to time. I know that we are not heading for the central station in town. I don't know where they are taking us, but there are no longer any other vehicles escorting us. We are alone and I think we are more likely to end up in a chiller than in the cooler. No one says anything for quite some time, then eventually one of the policemen in the front slides the partition window across, looks us over for a moment, and says to our guards:

'We'll be there soon. Everyone ready?'

The others nod. Then he turns to me.

'It's the end of the line. No hard feelings, eh?'

The van is roaring now, labouring along a twisting road which climbs up a mountain to some unknown summit. With every bend the tyres screech like children being flayed alive. We hurtle along a long, high ledge overlooking a deep chasm, until the driver finally decides to slam his fat foot on the bastard brake pedal: we have arrived. The screams of the child-tyres take on a desperate note, then stop abruptly.

We take to the air. The officer to my right is staring aimlessly, with his hands on his knees. He has taken off from his seat and started on a slow rotation on his own axis, gravitating – in the true sense of the word – around his navel. We look at each other, hand-cuffed together as we are. He seems as astonished as I am by this sudden weightlessness, but he has barely opened his mouth to form a horrified 'O' when a divine hand dispenses justice by pulverising the van in an apocalyptic crash. Some law of physics propels me into the air and from there I watch the vehicle breaking apart far below me, and shattering over the valley in a hail of steel and plastic. Having passed the peak of my trajectory, I eventually fall back down towards the foaming crests of an ocean of trees. When at last I land, the sky and the earth are swirled together in an epileptic seething.

II

I AM LYING ON MY BACK UNDER a huge oak tree. I feel no pain at all. Death does not seem to have wanted me. It didn't even try to bruise me or break the odd bone. I stay there for several minutes, contemplating the varicose outline of the branches against the sky, before sitting up slowly and looking around. The life-saving oak tree, now gnarled and venerable, grew up in a large dark expanse of parkland. Narrow white paths snake between the silent tree trunks, and stone ponds murmur softly. A low grey wall follows the trees around the edge of the wood, enclosing the gardens. A expanse of lawn set with big paving stones seems to stretch off into infinity in various directions.

I listen to the sound of running water for a long time before I find the strength to sit up, unscathed but weary. My right wrist weighs me down. I look at it. It is still handcuffed to the flying officer who has been reduced to an arm, an enormous gorilla's arm hideously severed at the shoulder where it now sprouts a bouquet of tendons and nerves. Pretty amateur work, I think to myself. Death often lacks the elegance we think we have a right to expect: it has little interest in the means, provided the end is achieved. A glance around reveals no other trace of police remains, and I resolve to carry this limb under my own arm, so that I can get as far as the parapet.

The sharp white gravel of the path hurts my foot: I have lost a shoe, and all that is left of the sock is the elastic. Pausing to make a brief inventory of my body, I realise that I am also missing my left trouser leg and every single button from my shirt. I decide to go on anyway and walk on the grass, carrying the heavy arm which is dripping blood down my bare leg. I emerge from the trees and go over to the balustrade. Far below the carved wall a noisy torrent carries away the melt-water from the mountains towering above me. I turn to look at them. The garden is halfway up a sheer cliff, carving a deep dark step into its side. The huge noble trees make quite a contrast with the grim black pine trees dotted about the arid scree on the other side. Way up there, five or six hundred metres above the cedars and the oaks, I can make out the ledge that we fell from – a fortunate fall if ever there was one.

I look over to my right and decide to follow the openwork wall which stands between me and the chasm. Paving stones form a narrow roadway strewn with weeds, apparently carrying on far out of sight. I walk slowly and every now and then have to step over a stream coming from some kind of spring in the under-growth. The clear swift water pours into the bottom of the valley with a crystalline tinkling. Time trickles by, drop by drop, as I follow this disused road which curves gently towards the mountain. I couldn't say how far I travel along it. As I walk I watch the mist gathering slowly with the darkness, swallowing the mountain from its peak downwards and turning the scenery blue around me.

At nightfall, a vast esplanade of grass and ferns finally opens to my right. In the centre stands an imposing building in white limestone and red brick, its roofline ornamented with a wide pediment of carved wood. It is a four-storey house, with rows and rows of tall windows looking out over the valley. It appears to be uninhabited, frozen in faded splendour and abandoned by the light of day. As I look at the façade and the steps up to the large front door, I can imagine receptions in the roaring twenties, with sequinned dresses and fob watches. I sit on the parapet and stay there, exhausted, looking at that edifice of days gone by.

After a long time I kneel down and drink from a little stream, then finally make up my mind to go in. As I walk over to the house, several huge black greyhounds loom out of the shadows of the forest, like escaped hounds of hell. I freeze for a moment, uncertain, then elect to ignore them and climb the steps. They home in on me at a silent fluid gallop, sniff me and mill around me, then follow me up the steps at my heels. I am not afraid, I think I've met them before, have looked into their glowing eyes in some dream when I was chased by demons. The largest of the dogs comes up to my chest. He has a fine narrow muzzle and a strong neck. His back ripples as he walks. He looks right through me, can see into me, because these creatures probably have the same blood in their veins as unicorns and other mythological creatures. I tear myself away from his stare and stand squarely in front of the door, which has no bell or knocker. I push it hesitantly. It opens in silence. The dogs do not follow me. Perhaps they are afraid.

I walk into the entrance hall of the uninhabited house. The plaster on the ceiling has peeled away in eczema patches, its fallen scabs strewn about the black and white marble floor. I can see a few empty rooms beyond, unfurnished spaces, dusty panelling and bathtubs turned green by trickles of water. In the middle of a vast hall there is a forged iron stairwell leading to the upper floors and supporting a monumental glass roof, through which the grey evening light seeps faintly. I walk towards it. The staircase also dives down into the ground and from the depths I can hear clammy dripping from some kind of cellar, and sobbing sounds, adult sobbing unified in a feeble, droning refrain.

For the first time since I landed in the garden I realise how strange the place is. I notice the dread that it distils in my veins. A terrible feeling of fear floods through me: exactly when did I start losing track of events? I think back to what the policeman said in the van. Yes, I've lost track of things, like all that walking, which didn't take me anywhere – just here. Those dogs, that sobbing. Where *am* I? Is there a telephone? No, I would have seen the over-head cables outside, and – now that I look closely – there isn't even any electricity. No switches, no flexes, no lamps, nothing.

Keeping my distance, I skirt round the gaping orifice, ringed with ironwork, which plunges into the dank entrails of the moun-tain, and head for the doorway leading to the back of the house. I see a pair of a large wooden doors with panes of multicoloured glass. Hope swells inside me (I have decided hope will be the last thing to leave). But they open on to the silent twilight, the forest and the dogs, which I can barely make out: dark movements in the shadows. Further away the track disappears into the foliage, which is already harbouring a nocturnal darkness.

This evening I am going to have to explore the upper floors to find food, somewhere to sleep, something to wear. Tomorrow I will leave, I will go home. I don't belong here. So I resolve to retrace my steps and go up to the first floor. In order to do this I have to pass close by the staircase, which leads down to the cellar. The cries have not stopped, mingled with sickly coughing. I dare not look. Who lives down there? Why the moaning? Why this unutterable feeling inside me? As I struggle up the stairs I tell myself that tomorrow I must find some sort of tool, so that I can get rid of this lagging arm. It is too dark now. I can hardly see a thing. When I reach the landing I go into the first room I come to, pick out a corner and huddle into it. After an eternity spent listening to the dripping and the wailings of the earth, it feels as if I finally go to sleep.

A moment later it is broad daylight. The blinding orange beams of the morning sun stream in through the windows and set light to the room I have been sleeping in. Everything else is pure silence. The house appears to have been deserted by its inhabitants and its staff, if it ever had any. Old newspapers are scattered over the floor. I glance at them, they seem to be fossilised by time: a copy of *Aurore* from 30 April. I skim through the articles of another era, looking at photographs of people who have long since been forgotten.

A sudden creaking noise. I look up, leap to my feet and stagger.

It is nearly thirty-six hours since I have eaten – and since I started dragging this arm around, this exhausting ball and chain of flesh. For a moment I picture myself gorging on it, tearing at it with my teeth, getting rid of it and consuming it, killing two birds with one stone. It would be preferable to cook the thing first though: raw meat isn't good for you, there are diseases, parasites. Sadly I don't have any way of roasting a slab of meat. No, what I need is a knife, yes, a good knife to cut it up. I go out on to the landing and call. My voice has gone hoarse in the long cold night and it cracks like that of a consumptive smoker's. I call again. No reply. Thinking that the creaking sound came from one of the floors above, I go over to the staircase, head for the second floor and look up. The glass roof dazzles me with burning light, drawing me closer. Just as I decide to climb higher, I hear the creaking again, from down-stairs this time. A wooden wheelchair is trundling across the hall with a man in it: an obese young man with Down's syndrome. I watch him as he propels himself along with his short, fat little arms. He looks at me, smiles and speaks.

'Good morning. I was waiting for you to wake up. I heard you come in yesterday and I know you've met my dogs. They told me. Beautiful, aren't they? They can read the hearts of people who have strayed from the path. You're lost, aren't you? Then, later, I watched you sleeping, not for long because we do get so many visitors these days, but for a little while at least. Luckily the dogs don't let them all in.'

'Visitors?'

'Yes, all the people sent by Ariel.'

He sighs and says nothing for a moment, using the time to look me over. While he is scrutinising me, I take a good look at him too as I come down the stairs, dragging the arm behind me. His little speech was hardly what you would have expected. I seem to remember that some people with Down's syndrome can develop a reasonable level of intelligence, like a wise child, but he is different: he is not who he appears to be. I watch his lips, which do not move in time to his words, his thick protruding tongue, the saliva dribbling over his Hawaiian shirt, the bubbles of it in his mouth, and the way he waggles his head as he catches his breath before going on.

'You must be hungry and thirsty. You've been on a long journey to get here. Follow me, we can chat for a while.'

His chubby little fingers grip hold of the handrails on the wheels. He turns round and starts rolling gently towards the double doors which lead out to the forest. He opens them and goes out. I follow him, dazzled by the perfect blue of the sky. To our left there is a small wooden lean-to against the house. I didn't see it in the half light yesterday. This side of the house is still in the shade and has kept the cool, damp feel of night time. He wheels over to the shed, following a narrow path carved out along the wall by the combined effects of time and his comings and goings. The five dogs lie sleeping on the grass. Huge creatures, shining blue in the light of day, with a white star on their chests. They look up and eye me as I pass. We go in. A table, a chair, a mattress, an enamel jug and a cupboard, which he opens. I shut the door behind me and sit down. He hands me a tin of cat food.

'The cutlery's in the drawer. I don't have any bread, sorry. Afterwards we'll see about the arm. Are you feeling like a surgeon or a mechanic?'

'More like a mechanic.'

He opens the cupboard again, closes it, then goes over to the drawer and rummages through it before eventually turning to face me.

'No, it's not possible. I don't have the tools. It's a long time since there's been anything here, you know. There's just me now. They only left me and the dogs, for the people who've... strayed, I've already told you that. You'll have to use the knife hanging from that nail.'

'Who left you here?'

'The answer to that is beyond your comprehension. Go on, then.'

He tilts his dribbly chin to indicate a huge, gleaming knife on the wall. I take it and lay it down next to the stinking meat I am steadily eating from the tin with a spoon. I move the food aside and put the arm on the table. Even completely drained of blood it is a strong, hairy, sturdy arm. There is a wedding ring on the third finger. I take it off to put it in my pocket. You never know. I compare it to mine. He had bad taste that policeman, a great wide man's wedding ring in yellow gold – no idea. Hardly surprising he was a copper.

I grab hold of the knife and examine it closely. It's beautiful, worn with use. The wooden handle fits in my hand, the blade thin from grinding, sharp beneath my thumb. I'm going to have to carve the chicken. It's Sunday. All that's missing is Mummy. I eye up the wrist joint, telling myself it's only a piece of dead meat, after all, then I concentrate on cutting through it, pushing down hard. To my surprise, the blade cuts through the skin and sinks into the joint. I press down on the knife with all my strength. Force it, push it, turn it round, change the angle, take it back out and stand on tiptoe to bring my whole weight down on the wrist, which gives way with a crack. There is no blood, just white fat tissue, grey tendons, blue cartilage. I look up at my half-wit host. A glass of red wouldn't go amiss, but I decide not to ask for one. It would wipe the smile off his face.

After several minutes of hard work I finally manage to free myself. The hand comes away from the forearm. I remove it from the handcuffs and throw the bits of policeman to the dogs. Then I plant the knife into the table with a victorious 'thwack', drop down on to a chair, pick up the spoon and carry on with my delectable cat food. In the state I am in it seems perfectly acceptable to sit in shivery silence, as if an angel were stepping over my grave; an angel gliding slowly, its wings rustling like the blood through my temples. I swallow and ask the other lump a question.

'Where are we and who are you?'

'We're at the Crossing of the Ways. I am the caretaker here, pure and innocent, the last one left. Everything here belongs to me. I am the one who shows people the way and gives them permission to go up or down the stairs. I am the one who greets and the one who sends away.'

'But who are you? What's your name?'

'My name cannot be spoken here.'

'What is this place?'

'You already know the answer to that question.'

'Listen, I've had enough of this weirdness! I want to get out of here and go and explain what happened. I want to see my wife and children. They must think I'm dead. I want the truth! I didn't do anything to that girl.'

'You say you did nothing, and yet you remember nothing. I have very little time to listen to your pointless justifications. Like many people who come here, to the place I watch over, you are still blinded by your own convictions and longings. Can you truly sort through what is in your mind and list the things you're really sure of? Do you remember that girl's cruel beauty? The stab of desire she inspired in you? All of those things are inside you. As for what you really want, nothing is happening any more. You have gone back to the complete blank of your previous existence, but that comforting blank no longer exists. Many, many things end here, and many things begin here too. Tell yourself that you have never been more alive than you are now, that everything is just beginning. Look at me and believe me.'

His gurgling, croaky laugh drives the last clear memories of that evening from my mind, leaving a chasm of impenetrable doubt. I now seem to have changed from an inquisitor into a heretic. I lean against the back of the chair and take one last spoonful of chicken delight (with chunks), savouring it slowly. I put the spoon down and push the empty tin away. He's right, I'm not sure of the sequence of events that night. I am thirsty. I get up, fill a cup from the jug and sit back down. He starts talking again.

'What about the other man?'

'I don't know anything about him. I met him at the bar. We had a drink together, chatted a bit, and we watched the girl dancing barefoot. My wife was sitting at a table with our friends. The children were asleep. The girl was dancing and – a bit later I think

— I went outside with him to smoke a joint. It's pretty rare nowadays to meet someone who offers you good weed like that. I think we also had half a bottle of Oban. We walked along the fairway. We made sandcastles in a bunker with a champagne bucket. Then he told me he had some really strong stuff I could try, some oil or some LSD, something like that. That was when we heard the sound. The girl was there, below us, naked and dead.'

He sits in silence for a long time, deep in what might just as easily be a short absence as a long contemplation. Eventually he speaks again.

'What you've just told me is a ridiculous fabrication, so obviously cobbled together. You can't possibly believe in it, because your being here proves that what actually happened was quite different. Anyway, you can't stay here. I want you to leave. You will go, and you can come back when you are at peace with yourself, when you have accepted the truth.'

'Come back? Why would I want to come back? I don't know who you are or where we are. Why would I come back?'

'So that I can get you across the river. But that time will come. Go now, because the storm will soon reach us up here. You were brought to me by drugs and circumstances, but it's not quite time for us to meet. Follow the path under the trees. You'll soon find there's nothing else you can do. You have to find out what happened that night. In the meantime you'll have to make do with your status as a Bastard With No Name, neither chosen nor condemned, an In-Between, a remanence.'

I do not understand a word he is saying, and I am just about to ask him for more information about this Ariel when a long, lumbering rumble comes up from deep under the beaten earth beneath my feet. I turn towards the little window. It is dark. The storm really is coming up. I look back at him.

'It's time I left, isn't it?'

'Yes, nearly. But you'll have to change first. You can't go in what you're wearing.'

A half turn of his wheels and he is by the mattress, taking some clothes from under it: a Hawaiian shirt, a pair of shorts and some flip-flops, which he offers to me with an appealing twinkle. I shudder in silence, and get changed while he clears the table. No pockets: I put the policeman's wedding ring on my thumb. Standing with my back to the door, I look at him one last time, hideous in his infirmity. He holds my stare until I look away, then he comes over towards me and murmurs.

'Go on now.'

I leave without turning back. The windows of the shed shudder to the muted rhythms of the storm. The sky is leaden, blinding flashes of lightning weaving back and forth through it. The forest shivers with electric tension in a constant rumbling, punctuated by crackling sounds. The dogs are on their feet, circling on the grass in front of me, necks taut, slaver on their jaws, framing their chops. They are the same colour as the sky. I ignore them and cut across the garden to the path which leads off into the under-growth. The dogs stream swiftly past me and go into the shed in a cacophony of upturned chairs and tables. I set off at a run, trying not to listen to their baying as they tear my host to pieces, nor to his shrieks of pain, mingled with hysterical laughter. The trees close in over me just as the rain begins to fall.

The gravel path describes elegant arabesques in the heart of the supernaturally geometrical garden. Here the scalding rain of the storm is transformed into thick shimmering layers, which smudge the contours of the cypresses and the box hedges, diffusing the effect of the serried lines and perspectives. I think I am heading towards the cliff, and the air grows heavy with mist, offspring born of the ground and the rain. I feel almost stifled, but the tepid water trickling down my neck bolsters my strength. I step over neatly trimmed spindle hedges, listening to the rain splattering on the trees, and the endless splashing of fountains and ponds overflowing in the downpour.

After a while the black cliff rears up ahead of me, streaming with water and froth, eroded by countless storms and marbled with age-old lichens. A steep flight of steps carves its way up this natural wall. I stop at the foot of the edifice and look up, but all I can see is a dark sky far above some glistening vegetation. A little torrent of water is bouncing off the steps creating a jubilant waterfall, inviting me to climb up. The ledge must be very high, beyond the curtains of rain and the veils of mist. I blink to avoid the constant drops of water. I am going to have to climb.

The ascent does indeed turn out to be difficult. I have to use my hands and feet to avoid slipping and breaking my neck at the bottom. I reach the tops of the tallest trees, then carry on beyond them, but I can neither look down nor even turn to look over the forest as I leave it behind. Any acrobatic attempt to crane my neck would undoubtedly result in a fatal fall because, without really knowing why, I am pretty certain there would be no second miracle. So it is without a backward glance that I leave that peculiar property and heave myself slowly towards an unknown goal.

After an hour, perhaps more, the cliff shallows out at last and the steps head off squarely to the right-hand side. I sit for a moment and rest. My fingers are cut, my nails torn, my arms exhausted. Only the flip-flops have stayed the course. I get up and go over to the edge, looking down at my strange resting place to get a feel of it in its entirety and to understand its layout. It is no good, the fog is too thick, stretching out in a grim, milky sea. So I set off climbing the steps again. They soon start twisting between piles of fallen rocks, which screen the cliff face from sight. I have to stop twice more on my journey to catch my breath and rub my legs, which are racked with cramp. The storm has passed and the burning rays of the midday sun finally break through the clouds. My clothes are beginning to steam as they dry. The steps have flattened out into a path through the scrub which eventually, after a long straight stretch, arrives by the road along the ledge. Here I am back where I started: things can now begin again.

It is hot. Summertime. Under the crushing heat of the sun the scrubland exhales a smell of resin and heather. It does not look as if it has rained here, everything is tinder dry. In the hope of hitching a lift I follow the road, a long snake of melting tarmac which winds its narrow way down towards Nice, affording a magnificent panoramic view of the bay. Soon this tributary launches itself into a bigger road. I ignore the give-way signs and carry on, aiming for the city. We have friends there, I might borrow some money from them. Then I can think about what to do next. I don't want to go to the police, and I hesitate to go home as I expect plain-clothes agents will be waiting for me there. If they catch me I'll have to explain a few things, which will be confusing for them and awkward for me. Who killed the girl? Have they found the wreck of the van? Where were the policemen taking me? 'You've done a good job,' the policeman sitting in the front had said, shortly before that cripple of a driver sent us into orbit around Andromeda.

I don't even know what day it is. Well, actually I do: the wedding party was on Saturday night... It must be Tuesday. In fact, I should be at work, in a white shirt, a tie and a dark suit, under the wan neon lights of the BMW franchise in Bagnolet. I think of all those gleaming motorbikes lined up in the window. I sell overpriced machines on credit to people who cannot afford them. Well, we all have to earn a crust, even if it means ruining our own neighbours. I like my work, I give people pleasure, or rather, I sell it to them at a high price. I like talking and the bikers who come to the salesroom are eager to listen to me extolling the virtues of the machines we have on offer. They love motorbikes and I meet people who are happy just to come in and drool at the sight of such polished perfection, even if I do sometimes have to bully them a little to get them to leave with one. When I say motorbikes, I ought to make something clear: I sell good big bikes, not asthmatic little boiled sweets you can ride on your driving licence if you are a grey-suited middle-manager with image problems – the sort of man on ten times the minimum wage who thinks he looks rebellious perched on his nineteen horse-power plastic chopper. No, I mean real bikes with a serious cubic capacity and two, three or four cylinders, depending on how smooth you want your ride. For as far back as I can remember I have lived on wheels: the yellow tricycle with a tipper bucket, the little red bike with stabilisers, the blue bike with ten-speed gears from Manufrance. When I was about thirteen I invested around 30 in an old Motobécane go-kart, which I dumped a few months later in favour of a 103 MVL: the obsession had begun. Whole nights spent filing the cylinder liners, honing the transfers, polishing the pipes. My life was suddenly reduced to obscure accessories: Dell'Orto carburettors, boxes of valves, expansion units. I threw away all my old beliefs and started worshipping Polini and Malossi, the gods of pleasure. The demonic attraction of speed had taken hold of me. Then along came adulthood, work, money, my licence and the big cylinders. My passion could be summed up in three letters which changed according to my accidents and my fickle heart: ZZR, ZXR, GSX (R or F), YZF, GPZ, CBR, RSV, VTR, VFR, ZRX – complete gibberish for all but a few aficionados. In the end I settled for the three letters BMW, more by chance than choice, and I made it my career.

It is in this meditative state that the ten cylinders and twelve litres of a huge articulated Volvo lorry find me. A mountainous hunk of steel comes to a stop in a booming medley of graunching and hissing. The deep muffled beating of its steel heart reverberates in my chest. For a moment I stand motionless by the side of the road, then I climb up the short ladder to the cab, a huge lookout tower perched three metres off the ground. I open the door. This massive truck is driven by a skinny little guy of about thirty, with patchy stubble, a crew cut and a roll-up drooping from his lip. Lorry drivers are no longer the beefcakes they once were, thanks to all the powered assistance they now get from the tips of the pedals to the tops of the wing mirrors. Still, this particular driver has managed to imprint his own, rural sort of atmosphere on the inside of his monument to Scandinavian design. Sitting there in his vest, with his Paul Ricard sunhat and his Paulo 89 number plates, the guy looks at me weirdly, stares even. I see a wave of terror flicker through his brown eyes. I hope he doesn't recognise me. They must have shoved my face on the front page of every local rag. A trucky's calendar full of naked women hangs above the bunk. I find that reassuring. He's not the type to read newspapers. I sit down and, for a few moments, revel in the air conditioning inside the cab, then I turn to him.

'Thanks for stopping,' I say, 'my car's broken down on the cliff road. If you could drop me in town that would be very kind.'

'Ah… Yes. Well… I'll leave you at the toll booths before the motorway. I can't go into Nice, it's not allowed. Are you lost?'

'No, I just broke down, I'm going to get a friend to try to sort it out – the distributor, I think.'

He looks at me intently, as if he knows me. I don't think he is taken in by my improvised fabrications. He puts the huge machine in gear again, still watching me out of the corner of his eye. I pretend not to notice anything.

'Do you drive?' he asks.

'Yes, who doesn't?'

'No, I mean do you have your licence?'

'Umm… Yes.'

He gives a roar of laughter which sends the whole lorry

shuddering off its smooth trajectory. As he catches his breath, he manages to say:

'Well, bugger me, and this lands in my lap. I've seen it all now. Perhaps the gentleman's a NASA engineer as well, is he? My mates at the depot will never believe this. Bugger me. Wait, wait.'

He opens the glove compartment and rummages through it, still keeping one eye on the road. A car overtakes us, hooting. He pulls out a disposable camera, points it at me and takes a picture with one hand, without looking in the viewfinder. He is getting on my nerves.

'Stop that right now. I don't want you taking photos of me. Who do you think you are? If you're going to be like that you can drop me right here, I'll carry on on foot.'

'It's okay. Don't get angry, my friend. It's just for a laugh. No, seriously, your shirt's great. Are you planning to go far like that?' he asks, the fuckwit, splitting his sides with laughter again. Just my luck. There's one nutter on the road and I'm with him.

'It's nobody's business but my own where I'm going,' I say, trying to be firm. 'I need to repair my car.'

'Yeah, right.'

I give up. We sit in silence. His mascots swing limply from the rear-view mirror. He wipes the tears from his eyes with the back of his hand. We have stopped talking and for some time we follow a very busy main road, which takes us on to a slip road to the motorway. I watch him going up through the gears with the technique and application of a professional. We carry on for a few more kilometres before he parks on the hard shoulder.

'There you are, my friend, we're here. No hard feelings, hey?

Hop over the barrier and go down the bank there and you're pretty much in town. Wait, wait.'

He's not laughing now, his face is serious. He looks at me again, stares into my eyes for a second, then turns away quickly. He reaches out and grabs a pair of sunglasses from the dashboard.

'At least put these on if you're going into town, as a precaution.'

'Why?'

'They go well with your shorts. I've done time too, you know. I can get those off for you if you want.'

He points at the handcuffs hanging from my wrist. They are the first thing anyone will see. I won't manage a hundred metres without being arrested. He climbs down from his cab and comes back up a few moments later with a huge pair of pliers. Without a word, he snaps off the wretched bracelet – mind you, I had become completely indifferent to the savage way it cut into my flesh. He nods his head to show that that's as far as his intervention goes. I leave the handcuffs on the seat and get down from the cab without thanking him or saying goodbye. He recognised me. There is no doubt about that, but I am convinced he won't inform the authorities – otherwise why would he have helped me? I watch him set off again in a great cloud of black diesel smoke, disappearing slowly into the distance to play his noisy mechanical symphony on some other road. I weigh up the sunglasses in my hand, briefly consider throwing them into the rubbish strewn along the side of the motorway, but eventually decide to put them on, just as a precaution. I hope they don't make me look too stupid. I'll have to check.

For nearly three days now I have seen nothing but psychopaths and nut cases. I need sleep, drink, food and normal people to talk to. I go down the embankment, which is little more than a depository for plastic bags and drink cans, step over the crash barrier and start to walk along a street.

III

BEFORE THE DAYS OF THE National Party, Nice was the sort of town that deserved to have a neutron bomb dropped on it, the main problem being the population's insistence on voting so haphazardly in local elections. In the architecture department, the Promenade des Anglais could have done with conventional bombing. How could a four-lane main road along the back of a beach have earned such a favourable reputation? Let's be frank about this, it's incomprehensible: pebbles that hurt your bum, mahogany-brown old women taking Micro-Rover for a walk in leopard-skin leggings, handsome hunks skateboarding in cycling shorts, girls with all the right curves in bikini tops and on roller skates, swanky cars, smart hotels... but not that smart: a poor-man's Monaco.

The problem was partly resolved when the principality was

annexed and brought in line with the regime in Paris. A few para-troopers and a condemnation from the UN later and the royal family were tried for tax fraud, arms trafficking, exploiting their position, violating gaming laws, being an affront to propriety and public decency, failing to discriminate in favour of French nationals and misappropriation of national funds. Their assets were confiscated and the family deported to an Instruction Centre at Saint-Pierre-et-Miquelon. The new order swept through the town of Nice with one swish of the military police, and the constant stream of suitcases with their patchwork of destination labels ceased. Chain bracelets and signet rings went out of fashion, and most company directors swapped their sunglasses and healthy tans for leather coats and an austere expression. Money drained away from the city and the surrounding area. The locals became more discreet, almost drab, and the town more bearable. A few people were incensed that the heirs to a seven-hundred-year-old dynasty could be treated in such a manner. Others retorted that they had enjoyed favourable treatment, having been spared forced labour in Siberia.

Anxious not to be seen, I cut through the old town. It is infested with tourists stinking of chips and sun-cream, but still has the soft pastel colours chosen by the people who lived here before the days of property developers, silly money and the Russian mafia. With those scourges now eradicated, I can enjoy the quiet charm of its paved streets, the stench of dustbins in the southern sun, the muffled bustle of restaurant kitchens, the darkness of dead-end alleys, the leprous walls and their flaky-pastry layers of posters. I take my time, ambling slowly as I head towards the sea, just beginning to savour its simple but indescribable smell. I know I am protected from the tourists by the design of my shirt, it is better camouflage than commando gear in a jungle. All the potential informers who, I am now convinced, have seen my face in the papers look right through me. I can well imagine some photobooth picture blown up to grotesque, grainy pixilation and plastered on the front page under the word 'ASSASSIN'. The photo would show a man with brown hair and dark eyes, like so many others. Of course, I would be the only person to think I was unrecognisable. I imagine the same photograph pinned up in every police station, every guard-room, in airports, border patrols, taxis and bus-shelters. I can see it digitised on the Internet, and I can also see my mother selling off old holiday snaps to the tabloids. Too much imagination, however, does more harm than good. I would do better to get a move on.

I go past what was the Hotel de Ville. Like everywhere else the inscription saying *Mairie* has long since disappeared, replaced with the now standard *Governance*. You can still make it out underneath, if you look really closely. The motto of the obsolete republic has also been erased, though not replaced. Over the doorway the Party flag flies alongside the national flag. What bothers me is that they are both disgustingly dirty. I turn away and head off, regretting ever seeing those standards we fought so hard for so neglected. I eventually arrive down by the sea in the full blaze of the sun. I take a deep breath and look out over the Bay of Angels with its endless to and fro of aeroplanes overhead. I start walking towards the airport, accompanied by the late afternoon sunshine. I have to keep a constant eye out to avoid being bowled over by some hip youngster on roller skates, or spotted by an agent. And I see quite a few of them, busy extracting the toll-taxes by the roadside, to the dismay of drivers caught in their net. No one chooses to be a fly in their spider web. The agents of the National Militia have new uniforms, wider and darker with lots of different sections and an impressive array of accessories on their belts: revolver, electric truncheon, standard truncheon, attack alarm, handcuffs, walkie-talkie, master key card, torch, Swiss penknife, fines book, whistle, map of the city and ballpoint pen (with four colours). In spite of this magnificent panoply – a sadomasochist's delight – the agents don't look as if they are having a good time with the motorists. I stop halfway, to slake my thirst at a fountain. I take off my glasses and drink copiously. The water is cool, delicious. A dog is watching me, a little white mongrel with black eyes: a nice animal. He just stares at me, motionless, then starts whining. I stop drinking and stand up. He turns and scampers off towards the beach, yelping frantically. I put my glasses back on quickly and walk away looking nonchalant but feeling ruffled. What's the matter with the mutt? I hardly looked at him. I carry on with my journey, plagued by questions for which I have no answers. Still, after all, I shouldn't really complain. If I can scare dogs off that's a good thing, because I've always loved terrifying little children. At one time I even specialised in murderous grimaces, often using them on those screaming dwarves who ruin meals in restaurants, running up and down between the tables. There's only one remedy for a curse like that: find the ringleader, stare him down and finish him off with something along the lines of 'I'm going to kill you, you and your parents, and then I'll eat your pancreas.' Then you turn away and take a mouthful, which you savour as if it were a foretaste of the said organ. After that, you must make a point of shooting them prickly glances, as a reminder to keep them nice and quiet till the liqueurs. The same method works just as well on a train, give or take a few variations. Children wind me up.

I soon come across a building I recognise with a façade done up with mosaics and enamel. I know I have to turn right at the next traffic lights, go over the crossroads and then take the hairpin bend to the left. Then it is the next right. Celia and Rachid live there in a lovely modern apartment block. Unfortunately for them, their apartment is on the ground floor. Fortunately for me, they are almost always behind their thuja hedge, tanning them-selves on the sunny terrace. There's the damn hedge at last. I'm going to be able to have a shower and some food. I can even hear the tinkle of cutlery behind the foliage and the murmur of their muted conversation. I call out quietly: no reply. I pop my head through the branches. A man and a woman of about fifty are having tea at a white plastic table. They are wearing swimming costumes and bath robes. The woman sees me, screams and drops the teapot which shatters, splattering boiling water over her legs. She is shrouded in a great cloud of steam. The man turns to look at me and drops the butter knife.

'I'm so sorry I frightened you,' I say quickly. 'I'm a friend of Celia Munuera's. Is she here?'

He stands up without replying. The woman moans and looks at her legs incredulously as the skin peels away and drops off in shreds. He turns towards her, then back at me, shocked.

'Who are you?' he asks. 'What do you want? Look what you've done. Are you all right, my poppet?'

'No!' she moans, tottering among the shards strewn over the ground. The boiling water goes red with blood.

I try to salvage the situation with my most winning salesman-patter voice.

'Sir. Madam. I can't tell you how sorry I am to have frightened you like this, but, as I said, I would like to speak to the owner of this apartment, Mrs Munuera, who is a close friend and who −'

'But *I'm* the owner of this apartment. It was assigned to me by the Ministry of Colonies years ago. What do you want from us for goodness sake? Go away or I'll call the agents. This is a violation of our privacy. Go away! We're not interested in your problems. I'll call them, I warn you.'

The man is scarlet with rage, hammering his words out force-fully. I assume from his tone of voice, the grey hairs on his slumping chest and the design of his robe that he must belong to some sub-species of manager granted early retirement. His wife has dropped into a chair.

'Do something, Pierre-Jean,' she says, gasping with pain.

'Don't worry, Marie-Cécile.'

'Listen,' I say insistently, 'this isn't possible. I came and saw them here as recently as May. Celia Munuera and Rachid Benabdera-mane. I don't understand.'

'Well, it must be because you're stupid. Please, go away. I don't know you. Look what you've done to my wife. I'll have you arrested − in fact, I'm calling the station right now.'

I decide it would be wise to beat a retreat, particularly as he has just picked up a microscopic mobile and dialled a two-digit number. I back away. A branch catches on my glasses and they hang there, swinging like a vulgar air-freshener in a car. The woman stops sobbing and gives a horrified scream, the man – who was red with anger – instantly goes white and slowly lowers the mobile.

'But... it's impossible. The Party said it was all over, that there weren't any more of you. What are you doing here? What do you want?'

'Oh my God, Pierre-Jean, I can't stand this. Help! Do something! Make him go away!'

I grab hold of the dangling glasses and run as fast as I can. As I leave I check that I didn't get the wrong balcony. No, I'm sure it's the right address, the right terrace. I'm absolutely clear about that. The apartment was assigned to him? Years ago? I don't understand anything any more. Nothing makes any sense.

I sit down on a bench a little further along, sheltered in the blue shade of an enormous palm tree. I am hungry. I need money. The situation has become considerably more complicated. I should have asked the man if he knew Celia's new address. Mind you, I have no intention of going back to question him. Celia left years ago? Impossible. I smell a conspiracy, something hatched by the police to isolate me and catch me out. Not very subtle. They didn't look very professional. But it is a possibility. The incident with the teapot probably saved me. Let's keep calm. I must eat and get some money. I could try to sell the policeman's wedding ring in some pawnbroker's or even a jeweller's, but I don't know my way around this town. Anyway, I could run into problems, be knifed or

God knows what (if there is a God, of course). The agents are looking for me. The safest solution would be to find a jeweller who buys gold. My stomach gives a long gurgle. Press on, then. I hope the shops are still open.

I am just getting up to leave when, without warning, three police vans arrive, complete with squealing sirens. I jump behind the bench and hide. The three vehicles speed past and climb the hill to the apartment building without slowing their pace, scattering pigeons and chip papers as they go. Through the slats of the bench I have an unrestricted view of the scene. The angle and the height difference have played into my hands: from where I am I can still see the thuja hedge. About a dozen agents get out of the sleek, high-spec vans, carrying truncheons and large sticks with a strap at the end. You'd have thought they were dog wardens. I don't need to see any more, so I run off in the other direction. I am going to have to be careful and, first and foremost, I need to change my clothes. I spend some time navigating through a crowd and try to melt into those great swarms of humans which pound up and down the streets. On the boulevard I spot a jeweller's claiming to buy gold and jewellery. I go in, keeping my sunglasses on, and the door has not even closed before the owner and his two salesgirls are eyeing me with contempt and disgust. Apparently I am not up to their usual standard of clientele. Never mind. I go over to the counter anyway. The manager abandons the peroxide blonde he is serving and comes round a display dripping with gold, politely blocking my way. He is a short bald man, squeezed into a tiny Third Republic-style suit. He addresses me in a voice that manages to combine anxiety, condescension and firm authority.

'Good afternoon, sir. Can I help you?'

'Probably. I sell gold.'

'And how much?'

'That depends on your means.'

'Right, I see. Let's sit down for a moment, then. Valerie, could you see to my customer please?'

Valerie rushes to help the old boot who is clearly distraught that she cannot find a suitable piece as a flavour-enhancer for her looks. I spot a comfortable black leather armchair and flop down into it with a loud creaking of hide, which could be mistaken for an enormous fart. After a moment's embarrassed silence I go on.

'I'm doing the rounds of all the shops with the same, shall we say, speciality as yourself. I'm playing you off against each other, you see. For example, how much would you give me for this trinket? If I like the sound of your price I could supply you with much more of much better quality.'

I slip the ring from my thumb into the palm of my hand, and hold it out to him. He takes it, looks at it, looks at me, puts a magnifier to his eye and turns the ring around with his fingers.

'*Robert and Viviane, for ever.* That's what's engraved on the inside. I'd rather not know where it came from, but the hallmark is still clearly visible. Here's what I'm going to offer you: I'll buy this piece, with its very dubious provenance, for the price of the gold. That's 40 rounded up in your favour. Would you like to discuss this offer?'

'No, 40 will do.'

He goes over to his cash till, takes out four 10 notes and hands them to me. I mentally thank Robert and his fat arm. I also spare a thought for his widow. I am sure she must have gone to pieces in her grief, missing those huge hairy limbs that used to hold her so tight, and that fat finger on to which she once slipped the wedding ring that I have just pawned to the first swindler I found. I leave the shop without a word, without even expanding on the hypothetical future deliveries of 'much more'.

I am hungry. A nearby Greek sandwich kiosk will do the job. I hide in a seedy-looking park and wolf down the filthy plastic food, then drink the water from a fountain to ease the salt burning my mouth. A young man is sitting on the bench opposite. I watch him heat up his little spoon and shoot his heroin. He's just skin and bone, with dead eyes and gashes all over his arms. As I leave I pick up the half lemon from my kebab, which has rolled over to him. He doesn't see me, he is far away now, far, far away. I eat the lemon: it's thirst-quenching and prevents scurvy into the bargain. As I come out of the square a BMW bike goes past: a model I don't recognise with a high seat and very low handlebars, a glossy bubble with grey streamlining, a sporty geometry powered by the perennial flat-twin. It passes me in complete silence – a silence I find as frustrating as it is suspect. Only on the Côte d'Azur do people have sufficiently bad taste to go for that sort of tuning. It takes all sorts.

Anyway, that's not everything. I need some less conspicuous clothes. I can see a man just closing up a second-hand clothes shop in a nearby street. I go and buy some canvas trainers, some socks, some beige trousers at 1.52, and a pre-stained white polo shirt. No underpants – too expensive. I ask whether I can sell the Hawaiian shorts with their puked-up design, the matching shirt and the flip-flops, which have riddled my feet with blisters. The guy doesn't want them. I steal a baseball cap from him in revenge and offload the beach clothes down a manhole. Then I decide to go for a swim, to get back in touch with the real world.

I stand in the water naked (with the exception of the glasses, which I will not take off again) and gaze at the sun, the wonder of all wonders, for a long time. It's the time of day when you can hold its incandescent stare without blinking. In the evening it finally reveals the full splendour of its perfect disc. As everything goes red, I watch it disappearing slowly behind the hills, while the din of car engines, horns and aeroplanes goes on around me. I float in the water until the sky is dotted with stars and the beach completely empty. Every now and then agents walk past with dogs. They are looking for me. When it is quite dark I finally come out of the water and get dressed, without drying myself. I am ready. Now I must go to Paris. I need to get home and try to make contact with my wife. That seems like a good idea. I have to find somewhere stable to get things straight. I won't get far with my remaining 18 and a few centimes. I must see Frederick to compile a list of his wedding guests. I must return to the golf course to find out what really happened that evening. My immediate problem is that I am on the street and people are beginning to thin out: if I am the last one left I will be caught. Right, I'll head for the station as quickly as I can. They'd better not be expecting me to pay for a ticket.

I find it easily because, like all strategic locations in the city, it benefits from a galaxy of road signs intended to bring those who have gone astray safely to their destination. I enter the new building, which smells of fresh paint that rasps my throat, and study the departure board. There is a train from platform 2 at 11.38, arriving in Paris Gare de Lyon at 10.08 in the morning. It's now 11.07, which leaves me thirty-one minutes. Duly noted. At last something clear and sorted. I cross the concourse, find the platform, ignore the machine for validating tickets and go as far down the track as I can. I decide to get into the front coach. Just as I put my foot on the metallic step up to the train, an authoritative voice rings out behind me.

'Hey! Excuse me, sir!'

I turn round. Five agents are coming towards me slowly, menacingly. They spread out. They have two huge dogs, both growling, ready to pounce. The man closest to me has one of those sticks with a strap at the end, determined to get the thing round my neck. Another switches on his electric truncheon, and I can see the tip glowing blue in the orange glare of the overhead lights. My heart skips a beat and, without thinking, I jump between two coaches. They shout out. I slip under the train and come out the other side. They follow me. I run along the platform. I can hear their warnings. I don't give a damn – I run for it. Shots crackle out. I can see the bullets streaming. I can't believe they're actually firing at me. I fork off towards the dark recesses of unused trains, hoping to find refuge in that maze of rust. They're still firing. The gleaming rails scud past under me. I'm running as fast as I can, running for my life. I make one more swerve and dart between two coaches idling there like beached whales. The agents have stopped firing, they seem to have lost me. I stay on the alert and walk a little further. It is almost completely dark, but I soon make out the beams of light from their torches probing every angle. By the light of the moon, which has just emerged from behind a cloud, I can see a ladder, and I climb on to the roof of a train. From there I drop down into a coal truck and bury myself in it like a crab. I'm going to look great.

I can hear the agents walking past in silence. Their dogs are sniffing and panting, then they suddenly start barking furiously. They're very close. They must have picked up my scent on the ladder and they're jumping up and down in frustration that they can't follow the fresh tracks any further. Muffled thudding sounds tell me one of the agents is climbing up the coach next to me. I mustn't move. I know that if I don't move they won't find me. It's always worked, in hide-and-seek, right from when I was tiny. If you don't want to be found, you mustn't move. There are now two green dots moving about over the roof of the coach, like two lethal fireflies. I'm petrified: they've got infrared vision. They're tracking me down methodically. Still, the agent hasn't actually looked in my direction and, after a while, he disappears. I hear him climbing back down a few moments later. Won again: nothing new with hide-and-seek then! I wait until I can't hear them any more, then wait a little longer. I climb down from the carriage, taking infinite precautions, and sidle back into the station, slipping under trains, running from pillar to pillar, and from shadow to shadow, from a pile of sleepers to a fuse box, sometimes stopping for several minutes to scan the deserted tracks.

I gradually make my way back to the platform, still intending to catch my train. There is no sign of any agents now. I am very close to the carriage – thirty metres, maybe twenty – crouching behind a low wall of concrete, catching my breath. When I stand up for the final sprint, the dogs are right in front of me. I'd forgotten them… they hadn't forgotten me.

They're barely three metres away, circling in the pool of light beneath a lamp. I don't understand how I could have got so close without hearing them. They are big, stocky, terrifyingly solid, utterly loyal to their masters. They are the perfect servants for an extreme police force: they know no fear, no doubt and no compromise. They are authorised to commit every slavering transgression. I think back to that poor sod in his shed. It looks as if it's about to be my turn, and that the show will be broadcast far and wide. Yes, one of the dogs has actually got a miniature camera on a flexible arm attached to his collar – the sophistication! Before I die, I'd really like to get hold of the sicko who wanted to make a public entertainment of my slaughter. The two dogs come over towards me, growling. I'm not frightened any more, I've had enough. Let's get it over with. I stare at them. They freeze, paralysed, whining. I take a step forward, they lie down on the ballast. When I reach out my hand to touch them they fall to one side, dead. I look up: no one. The dogs are well and truly dead, here in front of me. Their eyes are glassy. There's white froth drooling from their mouths. I stand there panicking for a moment, turn round, turn back, no one anywhere. What happened? My train sets off with a deafening screech. I jump over the two bodies, then run and leap into the carriage just as the automatic doors are closing with a swish of compressed air. I'm in. I look through the door at those two bodies stretched out in the lamplight, receding into the distance. I must sleep. Wash and sleep.

IV

I WALK THROUGH THE CARRIAGES looking for an empty compartment. As far as I know, night trains are the only moving dormitories conceived by man. This exclusivity means they are a habitat rich in strange fauna, fanatic individualists forced to share something that is not shared: sleep. The lone traveller who falls asleep among strangers never truly sleeps, always resists slightly, watching the others, wary of them, especially because it is night time and he is a worrier by nature. No chance of watching the passing countryside to kill time. So the micro-society in the train closes in on itself, a medley of young drunks, penniless students and women burdened with children. Many of them do not want to sleep, or cannot because the bunks are so narrow, because of the proximity of strangers, other people snoring, farting or chatting, children screaming, children crying, or because of their own impatience and the excitement of the journey. Mistrust of other passengers becomes a challenge to sleep, and this zombie-like population dawdles in the corridors smoking and watching the lights of the world passing beyond the closed windows. I walk through that crowd of wakeful sleepers as if it were a forest of dead trees. The toilets on the train are locked, I can only have the scantest clean-up, wiping my face on the curtains in the corridor. Oddly, my clothes are not that badly marked – and I thought I would be reduced to a charcoal-grey shadow! I spot an open sleeper compartment. There are some people just settling down in it, two couples and a child. The word 'people' has never been more aptly used. They are just people, normal, ordinary. At a glance you could discover nothing about them and hold nothing against them. I ask them whether the middle bunk is taken: shoulders shrug. I presume it isn't and lie myself down on it, my head towards the window. With a creaking of bunks the others get in to bed one by one. The lights go out and the train lulls me. It hurtles through the night towards Paris. I am going to see my house again, and my wife. My eyes close, at last.

I am walking through a grassy orchard in the horizontal rays of the sinking sun at the end of a scorching day. All around me wheat sways to the whims of a hot wind I cannot feel. There is no sound at all, but the heavy scent of the trees reaches me. Then I walk along an avenue of cherry trees, their branches bending under the weight of fruit. There is a girl in a blue and white gingham dress, the exact same colours as the sky, like a tiny shard of azure fallen to earth. She is beautiful, slender and graceful. I recognise her. I saw her hanging from the tree. She is walking towards me, her every move filled with a sleek elegance that constricts my throat. She looks at me and I know that I am the one she loves and longs for more than anything else, more than anyone else, and I love her and want her just as much in return. We sit down in the grass and I look at her body as she smiles at me and tells me things I do not hear. Then she tilts her head back and raises an arm to pick some fruit from the tree. I savour the sight of her white throat, reach out my hand and hold hers where it lies in the grass. The touch of her blinds me. The fields darken under the lengthening shadows of encroaching evening, then of nightfall − a night that soon grows old, its firmament illuminated by the last crescent of a pale moon. We have not moved, except for my hand, which is now in hers. Motionless, we taste the last hours of that ancient night with its ivory light that makes our skin look like the shimmering surface of the moon itself. I know that we are touching the essence of all things. I wish nothing would ever change, ever.

I wake in my compartment, surrounded by the smells of sleeping bodies. The train is heading north, inexorably. I turn my head and for a while I look at the silhouettes of the hills against the star-studded sky, and watch the light signals which occasionally loom out of the darkness as the train skims past them on its way. From time to time we rattle through a deserted station without slowing down, and all animate life seems to have disappeared. I go back to sleep and have no more dreams.

The noise from the other passengers wakes me in the morning. We are at the Gare de Lyon. I can hear its echoes around us. I haul my head off the pillow and sit on the edge of the bunk. I know they are all looking at me − mothers, fathers, children. They are wondering why I am sleeping head to toe like that, and wearing sunglasses. I do not understand why I have to hide myself, but I intend to find out. I haven't done anything. The agents are wrong to be following me, I'm innocent. Before getting off the train I count out my coins on the little table, then count them again: plenty for a pizza and a Coke. I'll save the delicatessen counters at Fauchon for another day! I gather the paltry coins, get up and leave.

I walk along the platform with my head lowered to avoid the cameras and the probing eyes of over-zealous agents. Strings of baggage cars laden with luggage speed past me, snaking through the crowd, sounding their horns at disorientated pedestrians not yet fully awake. I can feel us, a swarming crowd, checked over by invisible, penetrating eyes. I know we are being spied on for our own security by some anonymous and well-meaning authority. I bet they are at the end of the platform waiting for me. I can imagine them there in civilian clothes, trying to look like nobodies. There's the man leaning against the barrier and another one, there, pretending to be meeting someone. I saw them catch each other's eye. There are also those new agents in the blue leather coats, blander replicas of the men in power. They are standing a little further away, arms crossed, eyes half closed. They are on the look-out on behalf of the Party, driven by their desire to flush out anything that might harm the crowned heads of our New France. One of them suddenly takes a step in my direction. I turn round, step back into the train and unlock a door, so that I can get out on to the tracks. Another train has pulled up alongside ours and I find myself pinned at the bottom of a narrow metal trough, which stretches in a long curve in both directions. I cannot find a door which will open to let me into the train next to mine, so I eventually clamber under a carriage and climb up on to a deserted platform. I quicken my pace, cross the concourse and leave the station. All I have to do now is take the Métro from another station… why not Diderot, for example. I will get something to eat on the way. I step through the doorway. Here I am in Paris.

The weather is grey, of course, the colour of pigeons and pavements, but also the colour of Paris, its colour and its smell, a smell of grey dust, of rusted metal and dried urine, which gives me a feeling of elation as I walk up the avenue: we each get the special memory, the Proustian madeleine we deserve. Further on, after the railway bridge, which people insist on calling a 'pedestrian walkway', and on the right-hand side, is the little Chinese restaurant that my wife and I use regularly. That was where we met, fifteen years ago, and we still like to go there pretty often. The Golden Dragon is a discreet haven, a cheap restaurant where – for less than 7 – they give you more than you can eat, and then some. The food goes down with copious amounts of chilled diesel oil with a subtle after-taste of rosé, an experimental beverage and the only wine capable of giving you a headache without getting you drunk. The chairs are plastic, the tables Formica and the décor worthy of a school playground. You barely get your foot in the door before Mrs Li welcomes you with her imperceptible smile. You have to follow its every nuance, and not indulge in too much discussion about the table she picks for you. Once seated, you can choose your meal at last, but the menu is a Rosetta Stone, a conflation of crossed-out photocopies, Tippex, white stickers and

Post-its. The whole thing is covered in scribbled handwriting, some of it Chinese. It's a genuine work of art with its two red pom-poms dangling from the top, bouncing limply off each other. The human relic then suggests an anthology of Chinese specialities at a quarter the usual price: the perennial sweet and sour prawns and Cantonese rice, glazed duck and noodle soup. If you read the menu attentively you can flush out some really courageous offerings, such as Special Fried Noodles (a variation on Chicken and Fried Noodles), served in such vast quantities that any attempt to add to it invariably results in an 'Oh no, sir. Too much' from the manageress. It is actually true. No one except my wife can go on to have anything else after a feast like that.

I am level with the restaurant: Mr Li is no longer there. The scarlet façade has disappeared, taking with it its net curtains and its trashy lanterns. Where my favourite restaurant used to be there is a clothes shop with a stupid name and lighting brighter than ground zero at Bikini Atoll. I check that I'm in the right place: yes, no doubt about it. Last time we ate at Mr Li's was only three months ago – the wife, the children, a really good evening. When it came to the desserts, the owner came and sat at our table, we were the last customers and we talked at great length about his two passions: orchids and precious stones. I know nothing about vegetables or minerals, but my wife made them her speciality and so she made conversation. The Lis know absolutely nothing about motorbikes anyway. If they had been about to sell they would have told us, of course they would. I go into the shop. The designs on display look like nothing I know. The music playing is an incredible jumble of noise with a lumpy rhythm. I recognise the layout of the two rooms – it really is the restaurant where I met my wife. I go over to the salesgirl, who already thinks I am a tramp.

'Hello,' I say. 'I'm sorry, this is probably a funny question, but do you know what happened to the Chinese restaurant that used to be here, run by Mr and Mrs Li? Do you know why it closed? Has it moved?'

The girl is in her late teens, clearly well into the very latest fashion, someone whose ambitions – I imagine – are restricted to some local night club, and whose opinions are moulded by her favourite radio station. She is wearing too much make-up, her hairstyle is too complicated, her rings too narrow and her fingers too short. Her black dress is peppered with heart-shaped holes arranged cleverly to reveal everything without showing anything. She opens her mouth to reveal lipstick on her teeth.

'Well, I dunno. I'm new, but the shop's been here for years.'

I don't dignify this vulgar assault with an answer, struggling to show no emotion, sheltered as I am behind my sunglasses, warm beneath my baseball cap, none of which alters the fact that this comes as a terrible shock. I have a piercing sense of déjà vu – I've been given that line twice in twenty-four hours. I turn on my heel and leave the hideous place. I know what I am looking for. I glance along the street and see a newsagent opposite, a little further along. I run across the road. A car swerves to avoid me, beeping. I didn't hear it coming. I get to the metal rack of newspapers and just stand there looking at it, unable to move. I suddenly feel horribly dizzy. It sweeps through me so that I stagger and have to steady myself on the revolving stand of postcards. I feel chilled to the bone, blind and shaky. I piss myself, right there in front of everyone. I get it, it's okay. I really get it now.

All the newspapers show the same date. It's definitely Wednesday. But since that wretched night on the fairway to the eighteenth hole, since that night when we found the girl, twelve years have passed. Twelve years and three days. I look around me, stumble again, cling to a plane tree and throw up. Friends disappearing, restaurants closing, over-equipped policemen, bizarre modern architecture, motorbikes I don't recognise. I get it. A blank of twelve years and three days.

I start walking towards Place de la Nation. What happened? Where was I? What have I done? My mind whirs. The accident could have caused some sort of amnesia, or maybe a coma: I've seen stuff like that on TV. No. A twelve-year coma would have left physical after-effects and I have no memories of being in hospital or coming round or anything along those lines. Amnesia is more likely. Or possibly a mental illness. The shock of my macabre discovery could have triggered some pre-existing psychotic condition: well, it could. I've had strange visions over the last few days. They could be the after-effects of a much more serious state, which has left no imprint itself. All the same, twelve years of madness, of complete absence from the real world apart from the memory of some mysterious place and a handful of weird dreams. Perhaps I would do better to hand myself in, because I must have spent all this time interned in some specially adapted institution from which I have only just escaped. If that were the case though, I would remember being locked up. Twelve years in one room, with the same refectory, the same window looking out over the same landscape, the same day starting again and again just like the one before: I ought to remember that, whatever drugs they give the poor sods in there. Yet I have no sense of having lost touch with reality since the accident, even if I have experienced things beyond my understanding. I saw some extraordinary things, but I felt no alteration in my own perception, except perhaps on the night of the wedding, when I was completely off my head.

In spite of everything, I decide not to hand myself in. Wherever I have been for the last twelve years – an asylum, prison or some dream world – I am fine now. I know what is what, I know right from wrong. I am going to see my wife. She must have waited for me, I am sure she will have done. I know her. She will have waited for me.

On the way I raise my spirits by savouring the new city. It has been transformed. The myriad details which make up our daily lives change all the time, like the bubbles in a glass of champagne, so that after a while nothing is the same any more and you're drinking a completely different champagne. I note the shops that have gone and the ones that have taken their place. The cancer of hasty restoration has created ugly secondary growths in several places. Further on, the brasseries on the Place de la Nation have been renovated, but their signs have not changed. I treat myself to a pancake at the Bouquet du Trône. It has changed hands, but the leather seats have stayed the same. All is not lost. The Cours de Vincennes is still just as magnificent with its regimented lines of trees and the footpaths up the side. There are more traffic lights to make the traffic jams even worse. So the driver – to whom this prosthesis on four wheels is presented as an indispensable

expenditure and the culmination of socio-professional success —
finds he is quite incapable of using his car the moment he has
bought it. So what? All that really mattered was getting him to
spend the money. I assume that hasn't changed. I walk under trees
scalded by the polluted air. The women who used to sell their
charms under the chestnut trees appear to have been driven away.
Shame. I thought those girls pacing up and down opposite the
school gates had some educational value: nothing's ever enough
to cure the puberty blues. I walk all the way up the Rue des
Pyrénées to Gambetta, with its Governance building and its greasy
fountain, and from there I go down the Rue Belgrand (he was the
master engineer behind the Paris sewers) to Pelleport (wartime
general).

We lived in one of those red-brick buildings in Ville de Paris.
Luxury council-funded housing, with parquet in the apartments
and carpeting on the stairs. More than sixty square metres for less
than 500 a month. Not a hope of getting in there without pulling
strings: we pulled some. I sit down on a green bench to think, then
I look up and try to see something through the windows on the
fourth floor. The interior seems to have changed. My speakers are
no longer there. My precious 'Voice of the Theatre' speakers,
which had pride of place in the living room like two great wooden
barrels ready to unleash their stream of music. A good deal. A
friend got them from a cinema that was closing down. They had
been put behind the screen after the war and had stayed there
until those darkened rooms were gradually deserted and the
speakers thrown out on to the street. Impossible to fit into the lift,
I had to take them up the stairs and negotiate tenaciously with my

wife to justify installing two 500-litre blocks in a room of thirteen square metres. At the time it wasn't easy to get me to change my mind: I was a music-lover and obtuse with it — who cared what it looked like, so long as I could get the sound! So I set them up there and spent a good proportion of my spare time watching the bulbs in the amplifiers glow red while I listened to my music. That was all I did for years. Now my Voices of the Theatre have disappeared, but I know my wife still lives here. I can see her green and blue glazed pots on the balcony, the ones in which all plant life invariably perishes. There was one exception to this morbid certainty: the cannabis plants I nurtured every year, so that I could distort the slow-motion time of Paris winters to my liking.

I have been sitting here since early afternoon. The evening is taking a very long time coming, accompanied by a rain so fine it seems to hang in the air. In that damp, dusky mist the lights of the town blossom one by one to take over from the weary sun. Inside those brightly lit windows a different life begins once the day has died. I look over the front of the building with its coloured rectangles, the way you skim through a book of carpet samples. Here the crude white of neon, there the warm glow of lampshades, frequently the flash of televisions through net curtains, or the darkness of those who are not yet home. Throughout the building I can feel that languid activity familiar to everyone when we get home after work, fully aware that we have chased our tails all day and will have to chase them again the next, without respite, until boredom catches up with us, somewhere around forty. Or a bit earlier, or a bit later. The boredom of those endless lives.

It has already been raining a long time when I see her coming. I recognise her height, the way she moves, her walk. She is sheltered under a huge umbrella, which I also remember. My heart stops. She has salt and pepper hair now. My heart leaps. She's with a teenage boy, a foot taller than her: it's my son – I know from the way he walks. My heart breaks. A tall blond man meets them and kisses her. She didn't wait for me, she found herself another man. I heave myself stiffly off the bench and cross the street, heading over towards them. My wife's hair is grey before her time, and it really suits her. My son is tall, well-built, good-looking. He has the face of those youngsters who enjoy all the good things in life and take everything in their stride. No sign of my daughter. I am very close to them, the three of them huddled under the umbrella, laughing. The man is taller, more attractive and much stronger than me. He looks like a surfer. One of those men with the wavy blond hair and tanned skin nurtured by an upbringing on Atlantic beaches. The sort with perfectly toned bodies, white teeth and a determined tilt to their square chins. Those guys who gaze out over the sea with hard blue eyes and know how to make the prettiest girls laugh. He has a necklace of varnished shells, I'd put money on it. He must have sold my Voice of the Theatre speakers to buy himself a surf board, and their car must be covered in stickers from Waïoumi Beach or God knows what shitty place where they had such fun. I've been on that bench all afternoon dreaming. I should have prepared something to say. I stop in the middle of the pavement, blocking their way. They cannot get past. They stop and look at me. The man edges forward defensively. I speak first, even though I have no idea what to say.

'Hello, Albane. It's me. I've come back.'

She looks at me incredulously. I take off my sunglasses and they all give a start. I look at her.

'Please, Albane, help me. Weird things keep happening to me. Ever since Frederick's wedding.'

'Leave us alone,' the man interrupts.

I don't know what to say. I glance from one to the other.

'Leave us alone,' she says at last. 'I don't know how you got here, but you can't stay out in the street like this. They'll come. They said you were dangerous. You should hand yourself in.'

'Oh, come on. Try to remember, we were married once. This is our son, isn't it?'

I turn towards the teenager, who looks far from comfortable.

'You're Henri, aren't you? My son. I'm your father. You might not remember me. You were too small when I left... on my travels. Long travels. I haven't forgotten you, you or your mother, or your sister. Where is Lucy?'

'Lucy's dead, and you're not my dad.'

I stand there dumbstruck. My baby is dead. When? How? She was so little. Only last week I held her in my arms, seven months, almost eight. The jumble of emotions silences me.

'Right, that's enough,' the surfer says furiously, taking a step towards me. 'Now piss off!'

'Be careful,' she warns, putting her hand on his arm. 'They said he was dangerous.'

'We'll see about that.'

He grabs me by the collar and throws me into the gutter. He is very strong. I knock my head on the granite curb and feel slightly dazed. As I try to get up, falling back down several times, I can see them hurrying into the building. She turns to look at me one last time. By the light of the hallway, for a fleeting moment, she appears just as she used to, with her long hair, which has now gone grey, and her porcelain skin. Why didn't she recognise me? I sit on the bonnet of a car for a moment, waiting for the pain to die down. I rub my head. It was a bad fall. What a fucker. I didn't even have time to explain myself. She didn't understand anything. No, that's not it: she didn't recognise me because I must have changed in the twelve years I've been away. My baby's dead. I pick up my glasses, which are miraculously still intact. I want to know what I look like. I walk to the front of the car and lean over to look at myself in the wing mirror by the light of the street lamp. I can't see a thing. I wipe the condensation off the mirror with the tips of my fingers: I can't see a thing. I grab my shirt tail to dry it completely: I can't see a thing. I try the wing mirror on another car, and one on a lorry, and the window of a bookshop.

I have no reflection. Nowhere.

I stay on the bench through the night. It is pouring with rain now. For a long time I gazed at the windows of that apartment which was once mine. They passed backwards and forwards in front of the window, glancing out at me. At one point she came on her own and stared at me for several minutes. I haven't seen her again since. I do not know why they haven't called the agents. She was probably against it. I look at my hands and touch my face. Everything seems normal enough. At one point I get up and go over to peer in a wing mirror again: no change – there is not so much as a shadow or a blur to confirm my presence. I must be dreaming, perhaps everything around me is just a dream, the last vestiges of activity in a brain slowly dying in a hospital bed or on the edge of a precipice in the countryside behind Nice. Perhaps I am a madman lost in his dreams, sitting in the communal living room of some asylum, rocking and dribbling from morning till night. Perhaps all of this is real. Perhaps I am just a ghost now, an In-Between, that was what the man said. I only half listened to his nonsense, and I don't remember much of it now.

I am cold and hungry. It is dark and the rain seems to have no intention of stopping. I look at the soaking-wet pavement, which reflects the lights from shops, cars, street lamps and windows. The whole city lying on the ground, distorted, re-appearing as quite a different city, blurred and confused. Keeping my eyes down, I feel as if all the light in the world emanates from the gleaming asphalt, streaming up into the sky and splattering it with orange. I cannot stay on this bench any longer. I get up and head off in a random direction. It's not long before the mouth of a Métro station gapes at me in the rain. I am drawn to its subterranean glow. I go down the steps: it will be warm and dry and permanently light. I'm quickly disillusioned: I am soaking wet and an icy draught whistles through the huge Porte-de-Bagnolet station. I look around as I wait for a train. There are no advertising posters any more. They have been replaced by large mirrors in which I do not appear. At the other end of the platform a man is looking attentively at his own reflection. I watch him for several minutes: he stands there motionless, focused, paralysed by the reflection, hypnotised by it and apparently drawing strength from it… unless it is the other way around.

I will come back tomorrow morning to try to talk to Albane, alone. She can't have brushed aside everything we had. The Métro is coming, I get on, heading towards Châtelet, the last stop on line II. It is the most suffocatingly hot station I can think of. I will be fine there, curled in the subterranean, uterine warmth of that vast womb, waiting to be reborn. The stations reel past. People get on, travel a little way with me, then get off to fulfil their own destinies. We get to know each other with merely a glance, live together for a few stations, then part, never to see each other again. I still have no reflection in the windows, and I count the light bulbs between stations to pass the time. I would like to be able to talk to someone, to tell them what is happening to me. I would like to make all the people who cried when I disappeared happy by coming back and telling them I have not left altogether, but is there actually anyone who remembers me? My parents are long dead, carted off by stress and cholesterol, respectively. I have no family and so few friends. Of course there is Frederick, but I would have to go back to Nice. That is more than I can cope with at the moment. I am detached, incapable of feeling hurt, pain or despair. My baby is dead.

I change trains at Père-Lachaise, then again at Belleville. The Métro finally comes to rest at the end of the line, with a creaking of rubber. Everyone gets out, so I do too, and decide to walk a little to stretch my legs and dry my clothes. It is late. The nocturnal fauna are hurrying to get home or to go out clubbing before the last Métro. I walk down endless white corridors that fork off abruptly in other directions, and which are interrupted by stairways, corners, doors and sections that slope for no apparent reason. Sometimes I retrace my steps, thinking I recognise a junction, but everything looks the same. The station is huge, there are plenty of signs, but I don't want to read them. I just want to walk through the world's belly to forget, to intoxicate myself on white mosaic. Where is my little Lucy now? I drink some water dripping from a brass tap without a handle. I come out on to a platform. There is a space behind a row of seats so I lie down there. I am hot and tired, and I fall asleep on the bare tiled floor.

The last quarter of the moon dies away in a distant wave. It is dark now and I have walked along a wooden pontoon through a vast port bristling with masts. A series of lights, equally spaced, cast their faint glow over the jetty and obscure this nocturnal seamark. I walk silently along the path of narrow floating planks, feeling the structure warping under my weight, hearing the sound of my steps reverberating through the wood, listening to the water slapping against it and the halyards clacking. I walk on. She is over there, sitting on a pile of coiled ropes. Why did she go so far? Couldn't she have waited for me on dry land? I already know that my journey will never be over. I keep going, but I will never be with her. So I eventually stop in front of her, arms limp by my sides, utterly dispirited. She looks away. I would like to seduce her all over again, but she no longer wants me. I have lost her, like the others. The port has disappeared as the sea withdrew, leaving the sooty dark, crackling mud-banks and the gleaming kelp exposed for me to see. I call out to her, but she is leaving with the water. I would like her to tell me why. I would like her to say goodbye, to remind me of her, one last time, before she is out of my reach. She has gone. I am going to climb down into the deep cold mud, and I will carry on walking.

'You can't stay here, sir!'

I wake with a start. The station is shrouded in the half-dark of sleeping strip lights. A tall black man in yellow overalls is leaning over me with a little blue woollen hat on his head and a green plastic broom in his hand. Five others like him are standing in a semi-circle looking at me. A sixth is concentrating on driving one of those machines designed to pick up crap from the platform. He stops when he draws level with us, and gets out of the contraption. They lay down their brushes and cloths to move closer. They are the maintenance team, working by night to erase the excesses of the day.

'What time is it?' I ask, propping myself on one elbow. 'I just want to sleep somewhere warm. Do your cleaning and leave me alone.'

'You can't stay here. If they find you there'll be trouble. You've got to get out. The Métro will be opening in two hours' time. It's not cold outside. You've got to go, or we'll call the agents from the National Militia, and we don't want any trouble!'

I look at them, but do not move. They are absolutely resolute, right down to the zealous way they submit so blindly to idiotic orders. I have no choice but to return to the surface. I sit up and my glasses slip off. They jump back. One of them screams, the others gasp, appalled. The man who spoke to me takes a step back, he looks shocked but controls himself and, without taking his eyes off me, he speaks to the others in Wolof. His delivery is stilted, he seems to be giving orders and gets into an argument with the man with the giant crap-collector. They all talk at once, then the one who woke me suddenly raises his hand for silence. He leans his broom against the wall, turns towards me and comes over slowly. I am not afraid, but he is. I can see him sweating. He kneels down, reaches out his hand and puts his thumb between my eyes. His eyes light up like a child's, and he smiles.

'You're a Spirit, aren't you?'

'What?'

I try to gather up my disparate memories, strays grazing in distant fields while I tried to sleep. The events of the last few days come back to me in a series of blows. Perhaps I really am nothing more than a Spirit, a ghost. What else am I, if not a tramp?

'I don't know what I am. I don't know the word for it. I came back three days ago, from a journey. I don't have anyone left. I don't have a reflection any more. I want someone to help me. I'm hungry.'

He looks at me sternly, glances round at the deserted station, then turns back to me. His words sound like an order:

'You're coming with me.'

I get up and follow him. To reduce costs the managers of the intra-urban railway system dim the lights at night, plunging the stations and corridors into a murky half-light, which painfully exaggerates the unhealthy loneliness you can feel in those subterranean deserts. The main decoration in the Métro is still the flesh of the passengers. The cleaning team have gone back to work. With far from enthusiastic application they start their limp brushing and scrubbing. Perhaps they are beginning to suspect that the seats in the station were already past their prime when they were installed. While they carry on buffing, I follow the man who woke me. We walk along more corridors and down flights of steps which seem to dive endlessly further into the depths of the city. He opens a door to a service shaft. I follow him in. He walks ahead of me without a word. We carry on deeper into the hot entrails veined with pipes and cables and punctuated by large fuse boxes like glowing polyps.

I am waiting for him to talk, for him to say something to me, even if only to explain where we are going. Instead, he ensures that I gradually lose all sense of direction with every fork taken and every cross-connection negotiated. I keep on walking, helpless and exhausted. Now at last I can see what goes on behind the scenes. The walls ooze, the ground is hot: this is where the sap of the Métro flows. He opens a metallic door and we go in. It is a changing room. A white fluorescent bulb blinks for a moment, then sheds its harsh light over the room. Yellow uniforms hang from hooks on the wall, and there are cans of cleaning products arranged by colour in wire lockers. I notice seven chairs around a metal table. He sits down and waves at the chair opposite. I do as I am told. Then, at last, he speaks to me:

'You can't stay out on the street or in the Métro: you have to hide. You're a Spirit. You're lost, and if they find you they'll get rid of you.'

'Why are you helping me? Everyone avoids me, everyone runs away from me, it's like I've got the plague, as if I...'

For a moment I think about what I'm about to say. Yes, as if I've got a third eye. I read a magazine article about it: everything – animals and humans alike – is afraid of this third eye and will run from it or will destroy it if they can't escape: they would rather die than submit to its power. That must be why everyone who comes across me goes crazy. That power does exist: I saw those dogs die.

'I'm just a ghost, aren't I?' I ask.

He nods.

'Is that why they're all trying to hunt me down?'

'Yes.'

'If I'm dead, why do I still need to eat and drink?'

'I don't know.'

'What does all this mean?'

'The Spirit world didn't want you.'

'What will happen to me?'

'Only you can decide that. You ask a lot of questions because you're suffering the effects of your condition. I haven't got time to answer all your questions now. We need to get home before daybreak.'

'Who's "we"?' I ask.

'The other cleaners, me, you.'

'Why before daybreak?'

'Have you been gone a long time?' he asks me.

'Twelve years.'

'Lots of things have changed. The non-Whites are no longer allowed out in the day, that's been law since they came into power. Do you realise I was born in France, I went to a French school, then a French university, but I'm still not allowed to work where I want. So I work here, at night, to earn enough to eat. My wife and children lost their French nationality and went back to our country, but they're seen as foreigners there too. At least there you can't see it on our faces. Here the only people who are tolerated any more are the ones who can work. We just live alone and only come to life after dark. We're not allowed out in the daytime. Even my father's dead: the pain of it killed him. When times were good, long before he came here, he was an important witch doctor in my country, and then over here, even in Paris where he was well-known. He had the wives, the car, the house and the respect. They hunted him down when the Ministry of Racial Differences was created.'

'Who's in power?'

'The people you, the Whites, elected. The leaders of the National Party divided up the jobs when they came to power. There were seven of them, and they called themselves the Seven Governors. I'm sure you remember that well enough. At first we just looked down on them. That didn't last. They were powerful. They brought prosperity, but not for everyone. Now there are only five of them left.'

'What happened to the others?'

'Assassinated. That was right at the beginning, when the Resistance was very active. It's years now since we've seen the remaining Governors. They keep themselves hidden. No one knows where they are, and all we see on the global network channels are digitised doubles. You being a Spirit, it won't really affect you. You've got different problems. You're hurting.'

'Isn't there anyone left to fight?'

'No. Almost all the Whites gave in to the weight of their propaganda. I'm not the one to explain all this though. My uncle will do it.'

I can tell that he is relieved to have let off steam like that and to have described society as he sees it. What can he think I make of it?

I say nothing, I dare not comment, but I think I understand how things evolved after I left. I feel embarrassed and – to be honest – a little ashamed in front of him. I voted for the people who promised order and a new dignity. I voted, convinced that the others were steeped in corruption and dishonest schemes, that they were the incarnation of lies and deception. I voted so that I could be rid of the establishment. Everyone who kept telling me I had to preserve the Republic, the same people who took so much delight in that word without understanding it, the same people who mumbled through the Marseillaise which they had spent their lives so far reviling to make a living – they gave me such a strong urge to sweep the whole thing clean, to treat myself to a new government, to ignore history – even if that meant seeing it repeat itself. And so we voted, and won by a wide margin. The whole carnival of profiteers and parasites, the corrupt and the lazy, they were all brought into line. The same carnival which is helping me now. I do not have the strength to refuse his help, to spit in his face, when that is exactly what I have been doing since I slipped my vote into the ballot box. I am a coward like so many others, a coward and a profiteer, out for what I can get. I decide to profit once again from what I am being offered… there's no denying I've lost a lot in the last few days. I make the most of the opportunity.

'Are you taking me home with you?'

'Yes, but we're going to have to be quick, and you must keep your glasses on.'

I think for a moment before asking:

'Wouldn't you rather have become a witch doctor and taken over from your father?'

'I have taken over from him. I give consultations during the day. It's very dangerous. If I'm caught I'll go to prison. My father taught the art of seeing the invisible, that's how I recognised you. I can see Spirits and I know what they want to hear. Come on, we're going back to my apartment to eat and get some sleep. Then we can talk, but you can't stay long, you mustn't become attached to the living. You've got a lot to do before you can make your next journey.'

As if confirming his words, the door opens and the workforce comes in. They skirt past, as far away from me as the narrow room will allow. They are talking among themselves again, a language I do not understand.

'What's your name?' I ask the man who brought me here.

'I can't tell you my name, because then you would have too much power over me. Come on, let's go.'

He and the other men change, taking off their jaunty-coloured uniforms and slipping on their cheap clothes. They say goodbye to each other at some length before leaving. We are the last to go, heading back along the route we took. Why bury these poor sods in the depths of the earth? Wouldn't it make more sense to give them a locker-room on the surface? After many minutes of tramping through the tunnels we finally come back out on to the Rue de Rivoli. It has stopped raining. It is still some time before dawn. We walk away.

'Where do you live? Do you always walk home?'

'Yes, I walk. I live in Epinay-sur-Seine. It's quite a way, but we've got time. I'm not allowed to use public transport, anyway, or to have a car.'

64

I stay silent and walk beside him. As we head north along the tree-lined boulevards, I notice bustling signs of life in the shadows. They are there, all around us, walking along the walls, nothing but lone men trying to be as unobtrusive as possible, casting minute shadows as they pass under the street lights. I watch them – Blacks, Asians, Arabs – hurrying home before daybreak. The city is far from deserted at night: it becomes a different place, monitored by the police.

'What if we run into a patrol?' I ask, thinking of our own safety. 'Anyone who looks into my eyes seems to go crazy. I must be putting you at risk just by walking with you, and I predict the worst if we're stopped. Don't you want me to follow you from a distance?'

'Don't worry too much, Spirit. There are hardly any police on the streets now they've got cameras everywhere. Keep your glasses on and your head down, we'll be fine.'

We go over the Périphérique ring road, at this time of night flowing freely at last. I lean over the railings and watch the artery with its brightly lit stream of cars. He tugs at my sleeve and we carry on, walking alongside the A1 which has now been covered over with a drab, artificial park. We do not talk much, he has made it clear he would rather talk at home. The pretty lights of the city are far behind us, and the world is gradually growing darker. We now walk from the occasional lamp to a feeble street light. Rows of brick houses and weeds take over from the imposing Haussmann buildings and well-tended chestnut trees. The suburbs surround us like a dragnet, a black mesh closing over us without a sound, without our even realising it. There is no traffic any more, all the shutters are closed and there are no lights in any of the houses. We walk past indistinct walls edging an expanse of dark water. This is the Seine, flowing without moving, like a silent river of tarmac. We tread on nondescript plants breaking through the pavement on un-named streets, the vegetation smells of urine as we crush it underfoot. In places the filthy contents of a gaping rubbish tip have spilled out on to the street, forcing us to cross to the other side. Sometimes my guide even stops to rummage unashamedly through a fresh dustbin bag. He is in his element. He tells me he has no choice. Still we keep walking through dying, abandoned neighbourhoods. The houses have been shored up to stop them collapsing into the streets. The windows are walled up, making the buildings look like tombs.

Further on, beyond the rubbish dump, we cut across an area of wasteland which follows the railway tracks for several kilometres. There are rusting carcasses of cars strewn over it. We skirt round deep pools of stagnant water which have a worrying smell. I am just about to give up, to let him go on and to retrace my steps, when the suburbs gradually come to life again, or rather life comes back to the suburbs, re-colonising them. We come to the tower blocks, rows of white buildings like the teeth in a great cyclopean jaw grinding down the lives of everyone who comes within reach, reducing them to a bland mush. They are huge structures, the work of frustrated, megalomaniac architects attempting a desperate erection in the hopes of penetrating the skies which will never be accessible to such pathetic drudges. Each tower is a perfect copy of the next, repeating the same pattern of a few windows and an expanse of wall. When I look up I see that they cannot hope to rival the vault of the sky with its twinkling stars and ragged, scudding clouds. At the foot of these edifices there are great open areas of concrete and smooth marble, swept by a freezing wind which finds nothing to blow away. Everything is hard, icy, angular and abrupt. We might as well be standing still as we walk infinitely slowly towards one of these towers, though I could not say which.

Eventually, without using a code or a key, we go through the glazed doors into an entrance lobby: smooth, transparent, shiny clean. A strong smell of lavender-scented disinfectant stings my nose. The letter boxes are lined up like a mini reproduction of the giant rabbit hutch towering over us. Not one of them is out of line, not one mark differentiates any of them, they are neither burned nor broken. We take one of several lifts: no graffiti, no gobs of chewing-gum, no signs of damage, rudeness, pornography, rebellion or humour – so sterile it is boring. Times have changed. He watches me looking at my own absence in the mirror that someone saw fit to put in this box. The lift spits us out on the eighteenth floor on a landing which is an exact replica of the hall, except there are no letter boxes. I follow him to the door at the end, and the smell here is the same as downstairs. He takes out his keys to open the reinforced door which is just like all the others, with the exception of the gold number which identifies it. He puts the key in the lock and turns it, we go in, and he shuts the door behind me. The apartment is brightly lit: this is Africa.

The room is bare, as are the light bulbs hanging from the ceiling. There is no paint or wallpaper: everything is bald. The walls have the grainy, grey texture of construction concrete. For a moment I think there is beaten earth on the floor, but it is in fact the final stage of decrepitude of the carpet reduced to a dusty powder over time. This thin layer of brown soil is heaped up against the skirting boards, has accumulated in the corners, and traces the most-used routes across the room with pathways of compacted dust. The huge living room is cluttered with mattresses, and there are Blacks sleeping on them, apparently with their eyes open – eyes that watch our every move as we step over the resting bodies.

He takes me to the kitchen and offers me something to eat, which I accept. An old man is sitting in there, eating rice with his fingers. They exchange a few hushed words, then he leaves, carrying his plate. There is no sign of any electrical equipment in the room, which makes it seem enormous: nothing but an extinguished camping gas stove with an enormous stew-pot on it. My host takes a large dish from under the sink and ladles cold rice on to it. We eat from the same dish and without cutlery, dipping our fingers into a sticky, white sustenance without salt or flavour. He seems to find it delicious, and I force myself to eat quantities of it, then take great gulps of chlorinated water from the tap. I do not know when I will next be able to eat. When I indicate that I have had enough he gets up and goes out. I follow him. We cut back across the living room with its watchful eyes. The old man is asleep in a sagging armchair, his half-empty plate on his knees. We go right to the end of a corridor and into a cluttered room: dark pieces of furniture, a bedside light which is on, an unmade bed with a woman sleeping in it. There are several rickety shelves filled with toppling piles of books. He lights a candle and turns off the lamp, the woman does not move. There is a crack pipe on the bedside table: she won't be moving. He opens a cupboard and takes out an embroidered white robe which he puts on over his clothes. Then he unrolls a thin mattress over the filthy stuff on the floor. We sit down cross-legged, facing each other and he finally starts talking.

'I've brought you here because I'm going to help you. Then, when you're in the other world, perhaps you'll protect me from bad fate and spells, because you'll owe me a favour.'

'All I want is to know what's happened to me, what I've become, and what I should do now.'

He looks at me for some time, fingering a long wooden rosary all the while. Then he puts his thumb on my forehead again. I can hear the rattle of the wooden beads.

'You've done some terrible things,' he says, 'and I can feel the monster you're harbouring in your heart. There's some great secret, a demon, in you now. You have to be careful it doesn't take hold of you too quickly. What have you done?'

I tell him what I remember as best I can, and he listens in silence for several minutes. When I mention the complete absence of a reflection in any mirror he interrupts.

'You don't have a reflection because you're a Spirit. Your image is swallowed up by the mirror and doesn't come back out because part of your soul is already in the other world, the part the mirror doesn't reflect. As for your body, you have the use of it for as long as it takes you to finish what you've come back to do. The only way you'll be able to see yourself is in other people's eyes. If you want to know what you are, take your glasses off and look me in the eye.'

He draws the candle closer and leans towards me. I look into his dark eyes, and I can see a tiny image of myself: my reflection, at last. I move closer until our noses are almost touching. I'm not me any more, my hair is short and black, my eyes slanting and droopy. My mouth is half open and my thick tongue hangs out, gleaming with saliva. I'm the man in the wheelchair, the man with Down's syndrome.

'Is that really what I look like?'

'That's how we see you, but, for all that, you haven't inherited the Kingdom of Heaven.'

'What do you mean?'

'You have seen Allah, my people would say, but he didn't take your spirit. He sent you back to find whoever it was on this earth put this monstrosity in your heart, the demon I can feel smouldering there.'

'I don't understand any of this. What have I done?'

'I don't know, that's for you to find out. I don't know very much about Spirits like you, and I hardly understand anything about their world. All I can tell you is that, for years now, people who look like you – the simple, the misshapen, the deformed and the ugly – aren't allowed to be seen: it's forbidden. It would sully their ideal of Man's body and soul. That's why they're hunting you down, too, that's why they want to catch you. But you're not like the Mongols they got rid of at the beginning. You're like the ones that started appearing later, one of those Spirits they value so highly. You need to be careful because they want you really badly. Keep your sunglasses on, be discreet and quick, because you don't belong down here. Your time here is limited.'

'Where should I start?'

'You need to know that you haven't come back here to start anything, and certainly not a new life, but to finish your previous existence. I can't answer any questions about your life before. I'm afraid you have to find out on your own, and tomorrow you'll have to leave.'

'Why did the dogs die?'

'I don't know, but you can be sure that's why they're looking for you. You're a Spirit, don't forget that. You'll do and see some strange things before you leave.'

'Are there others like me?'

'Lots, all over the place. We don't see them or notice them, because they're discreet and they're sad, and they often avoid the living. Still, everyone like you ends up posing some sort of problem, and you have to be eliminated.'

'You're telling me that I'm dead, but I can feel my heart beating. I feel so alive, so lucid, even more than I was before, or that's what it seems like. Why?'

'I've already told you: I don't have the answers to all your questions. If it's any consolation, if it makes you more comfortable, tell yourself you're neither dead nor alive. Touch my hand now,' he adds, raising his right hand with its palm towards me, the fingers spread wide.

I put my hand against his. I know what my hand should look like with its veins and moles and scars, but I see someone else's, small, fat and creased against his large, slender black hand. This is the same little hand that turned the wheel of the wheelchair. I'm not the man I think I am, and I'm only imagining my body, still seeing it as strong and healthy. I now wonder whether I didn't actually survive the accident but, inexplicably, my consciousness has carried on to fulfil some obscure goal. Tomorrow I might go

and consult the archives at the National Library to try to understand the world I have come back to: a calm reassuring world on
the surface, but heavily policed and brutal underneath.

He talks to me for a long time, to the rhythm of the beads
turning between his fingers: flags, banners, parades, standards,
ovations, silence, censure, propaganda, bugging, suspicion,
threats, abductions, disappearances, denunciations, police, raids,
jailors, custody, interrogations, sequestering, torture, prison, exe-
cutions, mass graves. It is late into the night when we stop talking.
I need to digest everything I have heard, and what I have seen too.
It feels to me as if, with each new piece of bad news, I recover more
quickly. Like an athlete in training for pain and disaster I can now
cope with every trial as it comes.

He prays for a long time, then asks whether I would like to
smoke the hookah before we talk again. I accept. What happened
to my health when I parted company with my soul? The pipe is up
on a desk, posing as a lamp, which makes it undetectable until the
lampshade is removed. He puts it on the floor between us, takes a
folded cloth from under the bed and opens it to reveal a few
tobacco leaves which he prepares carefully. Then he crumbles the
hashish flowers into it. We smoke; my head spins. Outside, the
tower blocks stand smooth and white against the tormented sky of
a new dawn. I get up to go and look at them. They are rather beautiful in their own way. Proof of man's longing to better himself.
Over there I can see a goods train endlessly rumbling past, and the
grass I have smoked makes the sound resonate through me like
some subtle music that I continue to savour long after it has gone.
While the city is waking up for the Whites and going to sleep for

the others, my eye is drawn to a blue flashing light reflecting on the building opposite. I look down: eight police vans are parked at the foot of our building. I open the window and a gust of icy air whips away the warm smoke that was hanging in the room. I look down again, then turn towards my host and wave him over. He leans out, then stands up.

'You mustn't stay here, my friend,' he says. 'I think we're going to have visitors.'

'What can I do?'

'Hide: come on.'

He tugs me over to the door of the apartment and out on to the landing. He has a broom in his hand, which he uses to open a hatch in the ceiling in front of the lifts.

'Go on, get up there quickly, I'll give you a leg up. I can hear them coming on the stairs. Just don't move until it's all over.'

I put my foot on his hands and heave myself laboriously into the narrow, dusty space, then I lie down before setting the metal ceiling panel back in place. Everything is dark and quiet except for the workings of the lifts, which I can still hear, a faint thrumming that makes every atom of concrete vibrate. My unassuming saviour closes his front door without a sound, barely two seconds before the agents arrive, a teeming army of cockroaches spewing simultaneously from the stairwell and the lifts. I stop moving and hold my breath while they blow up the door without warning and charge into the apartment in a whirlwind of noise. I can hear tramping boots, shouting, blows, the crackle of walkie-talkies and the wails of people being dragged away in handcuffs. The intervention does not last long, perhaps five or six minutes, but those minutes feel like an eternity to me. At last everything is calm again, but I can still hear the to and fro of heavy footsteps under me. My eyes have grown accustomed to the dark. I can now see fluctuations in the light filtering through the gaps, as the firebrands of the National Militia pass just a few centimetres beneath my weak, overweight body. Two of them stop on the landing to talk, they have a lighter, more elegant step.

'Well?'

'We haven't got him. But he was here.'

'And now?'

'The Negro will talk, you can depend on my services. We'll soon know if it is one.'

'Of course it is. One more to worry about. Do you know what he'll do now?'

'Make trouble for us, like the others. We have to eliminate him quickly, and make sure Ménard is informed.'

There is a long silence. I hear the sound of a lighter and one of them drags on a cigarette.

'We'll get him, we just need to be patient. In the state he's in, he won't get away from us for long.'

'Unless he has help. Do you know how he could have secured hospitality from this black?'

'No. But we'll find that out too.'

'You have absolute carte blanche, as usual.'

The doors to the lift open and the two men go in. Their steps ring out on the thin floor, like blows on the tautly spread skin of a huge drum. You hardly need a degree in lateral thinking to know that they are talking about me. Why are so many policemen searching for me after all these years? How can they track me down when I look like someone else? All these police just for one guy with Down's syndrome? What are they really looking for? Why are they frightened? I wait for a long time. There are still a lot of people milling about on the landing. When everything is finally quiet again, I am so exhausted that I sink into a deep but uncomfortable sleep, suffocating with every breath, my legs buckled by cramps, sections of sheet metal prodding me in the stomach.

When I wake up my eyes are stuck together and I have lost all sense of time, whether it is day or night. I listen for a while and, convinced that I am alone, I lift the section of ceiling to have a look. It appears to be deserted. I decide the time has come to get out of my miserable hiding place, which proves to be a rather difficult operation without help. Hesitant and awkward, I eventually slump heavily to the floor with a great smacking sound of bruised meat. I get up painfully. There are seals over the door, barring access to the apartment that I know will be empty. I press the button for the lift, which does not come. So I have to go down eighteen floors on foot, taking the concrete stairs which spiral all the way down to the ground floor and beyond. Every now and then the lights automatically go out on a timer and I have to grapple blindly towards the phosphorescent switches, begging them to steer me on my way. I long for the true light of day outside, but when I step out of the building I am blinded by such a cruelly bright sun that I have to turn away and protect my eyes, which are prickling with stars. I left the sunglasses up there, on the kitchen table. I remember taking them off to eat the rice. Never mind. I lower my head and start walking, crossing the huge paved desert. Nothing moves, there is no more life here during the day than there is at night, despite the close grouping of these human silos erected to the glory of sleep. Eventually an imposing flight of white steps deposits me in a buzzing street of shops where retired couples are shopping in a happy and ethnically correct crowd.

I spot a stand of sunglasses inside a little newsagents. I go in, my eyes lowered, take a large, dark pair and put them on. At last I can look up and glance around: 'EXCELLENT RESULTS' proclaims one of the newspapers in a headline five columns wide. I cannot help smirking. No one seems to have noticed me, except for the shop owner, who is clearly waiting for me to pay. The thieving bitch only leaves me with 1.62. I buy a Mars bar with what is left and go out with a few coppers in my hand and a factory-made delicacy in my mouth.

I must get back in to Paris. I need to find a newspaper archive and read the papers of the time. Who handled the enquiry? What did they find? Who were the so-called agents who took me away? I should be able to contact one of the journalists who wrote the whole business up. I walk aimlessly until a huge road sign points me in the direction of central Paris. It's a long way. I'm going to wear out my shoes unless I can find a Métro station. I've finished my Mars bar. I'm thirsty and I don't know where to go. Suddenly, Providence smiles on me.

V

In front of me, idling quietly, is a gleaming moped. It is giving off a cloud of blue smoke and an irritating rattling sound. The whole contraption flashes magnificently in the bright sunlight, with its leather saddle bags, its wire basket of vegetables on the luggage rack and its string bag of shopping hanging from the handlebar. The little beauty is waiting patiently for its master who is emerging slowly from the butcher's shop. He is an old man with sparse white hair, wearing carpet slippers and using both hands to carry a package of meat wrapped in pink and white checked paper. He probably met this wonderful machine in the early days of his working life. He the penniless little pen-pusher, she the virginal moped fresh from the factory. They have not left each other since. She took him to work throughout his career, through those misty October mornings and the lashing March rains, ever willing, never failing. In return, he pampered her, polished her and looked after her so that her chrome never lost its dazzle and her brake light always flashed brightly in the dark. They have become one and have been for so long that they have forgotten that Time always separates those who love each other. I barge past him, knocking him over, and hop on to the machine, twisting the throttle. The engine starts up devastatingly slowly. The old man is sitting on the ground, gathering a crowd of passers-by with his wailing, and I have to pedal frantically to gather speed. Before I turn at the end of the street, I catch sight of the butcher in the wing mirror, he is standing in his blood-splattered apron gesticulating in my direction with a meat cleaver in one hand: I'll never be a customer of his.

I head south, towards the sun, towards Paris, trying my best to retrace the journey through the rows of poor, downtrodden streets, which look no more cheerful now in the harsh light of a sun without warmth. I go into the capital through the Porte d'Asnière, having made a few detours without realising it and taken a few liberties with the route which was meant to take me straight to Porte de la Chapelle. I decide to make the most of this because I do not know if I will ever see this beautiful part of the city again. Now that the sun is sinking do I dare grant myself a foolish moment of pleasure, a taste of the joy I once knew? I decide to go up the Avenue de Wagram on my modest vehicle. Let it not be written that I did not hurtle down the Champs Elysées on that contraption. I lean forward and pedal again, until I am doing more than forty kilometres an hour as I hit the Place de l'Etoile, cutting across all the traffic, from the pizza delivery boy to the coach full of tourists, forcing my humble mount close in to the rails. I want to achieve some hypothetical sense of revolt to propel me, lowly traveller that I am, on to the most beautiful trajectory in the universe, the route I take between the rows of cars on those thrumming paving stones. I ride on down the prestigious avenue surrounded by all that money splashed about by people who have no other way of shining, and I feel quite drunk by the time I cross the Place de la Concorde, the wind in my hair and a smile on my lips. I take the bus lane along the Tuileries Gardens and go up on to the pavement as I run parallel to the Seine. Then I cut the engine and freewheel under the trees. I lean the bike against a wall and stand for a moment, watching the mud-coloured waters trundling dead tourists up and down in ugly boats. The sun peeps through the foliage of the tall trees, mottling me with moving patches of light.

I stay there for a moment, recovering from my exhilaration, before deciding to learn a thing or two about the bike's owner. The string bag on the handlebar is empty. I fold it and lay it carefully on the wall. Then I unclip the two blue bungees holding the wire basket on the luggage rack: inside I find a shiny aubergine, five strong-smelling leeks and two huge courgettes. I throw the lot into the Seine, including the basket. I no longer have the strength or the time for that sort of thing. From now on I have to be quick. It would have been more sensible to have carried out this inspection on a piece of wasteland rather than here, among the crowds and the traffic. Next I open the saddle bags, which spoil me with a delectable abundance: a really crusty half baguette, a really strong saucisson, a really ripe camembert, a bag of little red potatoes whose exact name I cannot remember, but, best of all, the old man's wallet. The owner's name is Emile Lucien Faure and he lives at 11, Rue de Paris in Epinay. Judging by his date of birth he is coming up for seventy-seven and his birthday is on the thirteenth of June. Slightly dismayed, I contemplate the silicon chip in the corner of the gentleman's ID card. The spuds go for a bath, and I make myself a snack with the rest. The old boy has his National Party card, which I keep safe. It bears no photograph or date of birth, and I have a pretty strong feeling it will prove useful. The really good news is that the wallet is bulging with a big wad of bank notes. That's a failing typical of old boys like him, taking 600 to go and do a bit of shopping. What do they think they're going to buy? I also hang on to the cheque book. It's bad luck for the naïve shopkeepers who will become my victims, the sort who have carefully filled his stubs in for him, as is proved by the number of different handwritings.

In this firework display of cash the old man's credit card is the triumphant finale, given that it has a Post-it stuck to it with the PIN number on it. I must withdraw some cash quickly, before he makes any objection. I'm going to make the poor bugger pay dearly for the fact that he went to the butcher's with just a purse of small change. I think he'll be regretting that hundred grams of minced steak for a long time – 'Because you see, Mr Louis, with the state of my teeth, it's the only thing I can manage now.'

With the moped on its stand, I turn the pedals a few times to get the engine going full throttle again, because the beast is still good and warm. The little beauty splutters and launches into its two-time melody. I set off again, relieved of a few vegetables and very rich. At the first cash machine I find I take out 700 without even getting off or cutting the engine, and these are soon followed by another 700. The third cash machine confiscates the card. Damn. I disappear into a street alongside the Samaritaine building and head straight for Les Halles, hoping not to come across any patrols of law enforcers who, I have absolutely no doubt, are closing in with the ferocity of piranhas on that cash machine and its little slice of incarcerated plastic.

I abandon the glorified sewing machine against the Fontaine des Innocents, without a chain or a padlock. The whole area around Les Halles has always exercised a morbid fascination over me, a feeling of desire mingled with fear. I have no memories of this gigantic shopping mall other than the uncomfortable feeling it inspires in me. This time, yet again, as I head towards it, I am gripped by an obscure impression of approaching a hive that has been ripped open, a sort of anthill spewing out its teeming armies and savage packs, all watching me with hostile eyes that are dedicated to exposing my weaknesses for all to see and ridicule. The worst of it is underground. The bulk of this terrible force is not on the surface but in the arcades beneath: legions of tramps, armies of down-and-outs, platoons of punks and rappers in formation. An acute feeling of fear stabs through me, a fear of crowds, a fear of exposing myself to others, a certainty that the population which infests this monstrous rabbit warren is bad, full of evil thoughts, seeking out evil, reverberating to its rhythms, finding it and doing it.

At the top of the escalators there is a large backlit sign showing a map of the various levels. I formulate my request with the help of a touch-screen smudged with greasy fingerprints. I have an answer: there is a cyber-café on level 2. I want information and I'm going to get it. Next to me a woman and two men are all making telephone calls, looking at their reflections in an empty old advertising hoarding. All three of them have their noses practically rammed up against the glass. City types are weird, I think, before disappearing into the western entrance.

The escalator deposits me in the depths of the earth, bathed in a brightness as artificial as it is endless. Here, the crowd is not quite what it was. It seems that the State, or some annexed department, has worked hard to ensure that the Caucasian is the only race admitted. I notice for the first time that a good many people like myself have bleached their hair blond: fashion has gone for the Nordic look, I have no trouble imagining why. My brown eyes turn away from this pitiful new world, and gaze at the luxurious window displays. This swanky subterranean street boasts a series of different shops whose gleaming windows compete with each other to be the most glossy and transparent. I start walking along the street, not that I am any more interested in fashion, sport or furnishings than I was before, but because the cyber-café is on the corner. The old-style façade – all varnished wood and small-pane windows – is a stark contrast to the others I have seen along the way. White muslin curtains hang across the doorway and a metal sign suspended from two chains announces the mood: 'CYBER VILLAGE: TECHNOLOGY AND TRADITION'. Fine, I go in. There is neither an automatic door nor a doorman. You have to open the door with a real handle and close it again behind you. The atmosphere is warm and soothing, and the décor has an old-fashioned farmhouse look: floor tiles, wooden tables and benches, gingham tablecloths. The whole effect is brightened by the gleam of a dozen computer screens.

I make for the bar and ask for the computer at the back, between the false chimney and the polyurethane wine barrel. The man must be about fifty. His grey hair is tied in a ponytail and he is wearing jeans and a black leather waistcoat. He takes out a register and asks me for some form of ID. I pretend to have forgotten, rummage through my pockets, and eventually wave the Party card under his nose. He makes a note of the information on it. I ask him to bring a cup of coffee to my table, then I go and sit down.

The system has not really changed, it is just smoother and quicker, and the screen is polluted by advertising that pops up constantly. It connects at lightning speed and the images are complex and richly coloured. I do a lot of research, using various search engines, and eventually access the site of an Italian who 'collects' horrific murders, carefully listing and classifying them. His pages catalogue several thousand abominable crimes – some solved, others not – with links by date, place, victim's name, assassin's name and type of weapon used. The scope of the facts is impressive and readily accessible, and I am amazed this sort of site hasn't been banned. The sugar from my first coffee has not dried in the bottom of the cup before I order another, still typing information into the empty boxes. The site was last up-dated more than ten years ago which probably means that, even though it has somehow slipped through the net, its creator has been hauled out of the water and put away. Another list scrolls up: I see the line referring to my murder – there, in the middle of the screen, the date, the place, my name. The strength drains out of me, the mouse weighs a ton. Unable to resist, I move the cursor and click on the word 'Details'.

The barefoot girl was called Agnès Bouteille. She was thirty-one. She died of wounds inflicted with a razor and a crowbar. It is assumed I am her murderer. My name is written there in big bold blue letters amid the faint black of the rest of the text. I activate the hypertext link, which produces a file with first names, date of birth, date of death (I have a date of death! I can't believe what I'm reading – they have a date for my death!), qualifications, criminal record and psychiatric background. There is even a small photograph. I am completely unrecognisable, of course. I remember that picture, I needed it for the next stage of my training when I was eighteen, and I got it from a photo booth in the Métro station at Saint-Michel. When the strip of moist pictures dropped into the receptacle I thought I looked like an Afghan rebel. I still think that, seeing the picture again, even though my appearance is now completely different. I learn what I already know: the alleged assassin, arrested at his victim's feet, died when the police van taking him to Nice for questioning crashed. It is assumed that a violent fight broke out between the frenzied killer and the agents of the National Militia, causing the driver to lose control of the vehicle. No mention is made, mind you, of the ridiculous place – if, indeed, it exists at all – where the debris of the van was actually found. Somewhere a very long way from the road into central Nice, I can confirm that. Nothing either about the man who was with me and who cannot have been any less of a suspect than me. The brief text refers to another site: the *Nice-Matin* newspaper.

That site is closed. I was pretty sure it would be, so I give up and retrace my steps.

For a few minutes I entertain myself learning the modus operandi of my fellow psychopaths. The world is over-populated with demonic assassins, poisoners, butchers, stranglers and hit-men. There is even a Russian who kills people with sulphuric acid; thirty-nine girls, the oldest of them not yet sixteen. I can forget it. I'm just a lightweight when it comes to doing people in. Me with my pathetic Stanley knife and my fence post. Another link sends me to a different site, a Chilean one this time, which offers free access to the archives of *Nice-Matin* – I can't imagine why.

The whole business is dealt with in three articles which appeared in the back pages over a period of three weeks. Here, I learn that I am presumed to be the killer and I died when I crashed the van having, God knows how, taken over the controls. The only source cited is Emile Lefort, the superintendent who headed the enquiry. I also find the name of the club where the wedding reception was held: Brandebois Golf Club. I had forgotten the name. After the ceremony at the chapel in the woods, my wife and I followed the car in front of us, not paying any attention to the names of the places or which way we went. After that I had far too much to drink and smoke to remember anything at all. This little reminder is very welcome: Brandebois Golf Club. Such a musical sounding name it makes you want to marry off your children! It has a nice ring to it, you can just picture a bar there, where people lounge in deep leather armchairs boasting to a selection of ghastly but very rich golfers who will never improve their game – in spite of the fortunes spent on private lessons and driving ranges –

because they are devoid of humility. The quality of the game is hardly important, the place is perfect for playing with other thrusting upstarts, and comparing address books: tacky showbiz starlets, tyrannical and dishonest company directors, pathetic gossips and tat salesmen. Brandebois Golf Club: a name I will not forget a second time.

The two other articles are, as far as I can see, just a couple of paragraphs roughly thrown together by some work-experience girl under pressure. The first gives the results of the autopsy, which produced no more information than a half-wit could have assessed with the naked eye: the lovely creature died of blood loss, bled completely white after having her skull smashed with a metal bar – this having been found leaning against the tree. The evisceration was carried out pre-mortem, as were the cranial fractures. The hanging was a little post-mortem extravagance, probably done with the aesthetics of the scene in mind. The third and final article refers to the analysis of the wreckage of the police van, from which nothing of any importance emerged, the conclusion being that all the occupants perished. End of enquiry. The final sentences of this article are devoted to the exceptional dedication of the agents of the New National Militia, who risk their lives every day for our safety, having to deal with the lowliest individuals in our corrupt society, blah blah blah. When exactly are journalists going to give up this sort of Manichean moralising? The agents who took me away were no choirboys, and their deaths leave me completely indifferent. No, all things considered, I think they deserved what they got. I almost derive pleasure from it, without any feelings of guilt. I do not know whether they have come back like me, so that they too can finish one last task, or whether they are burning, consumed by the cruel flames of a Hell that shows no mercy as it dispenses justice. Maybe I'll have to take them more seriously soon. Perhaps they're already here looking for me, hoping to make me pay for their premature deaths. Hey, what do you think, Robert? Your Viviane, did she give you the same sort of welcome I got from Albane? What's the name of the man who's taken your place in her arms? Weren't we innocent, the two of us, Robert? Who is it who's playing with our deaths, having already played with our lives?

After a while, I trace the name of the author of these three rather lightweight articles: one Manuel Fangiolini. His investigative work into the affair is at best very mediocre. Who was the murdered girl? Who was this young husband and father who suddenly became an assassin without any motive? Why there? Why the savage butchery?

I ask to use the telephone and order a third cup of coffee. They bring me an espresso and a mobile. Directories give me the number for the newspaper, and I ring them. Vivaldi answers after two rings, banging on at me with his *Autumn*. When I get the girl on the switchboard I ask to speak to Manuel Fangiolini. She cannot find him on her lists, but she puts me through to editorial. Vivaldi plays his ten-second loop at me again, exactly eighteen times, before being cut off by a man's voice.

'Editorial.'

I don't like the sound of this anonymous voice issuing from some distant mouth and transformed into electronic quivers. I can imagine the catarrh in his throat and the freshly bleached smell of the office he occupies with such pride – such pride he doesn't even introduce himself.

'Hello. I'm Steve Harvey, French correspondent for the *Chicago Herald*, and I'd like to speak to Fangiolini. I have some information for him for the paper.'

The voice pauses for a moment. Its owner must be thinking, and he does not think aloud. Then the voice reproduces the thought word for word:

'There isn't a Fangiolini here.'

'You must be joking, aren't you, Manuel has always worked there. Come on, put me through to the editor.'

Vivaldi tortures me for several minutes. I am sent back to the switchboard and I ask again to speak to the editor. I am injected with another dose of Venetian violins, but in vain, I come tumbling back to the switchboard: the editor's line is engaged. The woman gives me the choice between calling back and waiting. I would rather have my Vivaldi suppository straight away. So *Autumn* it is, ad nauseam. Eventually, a man answers:

'Leporce, what is it?'

Don't say too much, do say it right. I serve him up the same pitch:

'Hello, I'm Steve Harvey, French correspondent for the *Chicago Herald*. I really need to speak to Mr Fangiolini. I have some very important information for him.'

'Fangiolini? Fangiolini... Fangiolini! Manuel Fangiolini. He doesn't work here any more, he retired about – now let me think... a good ten years ago, at least. It was before Global Network bought us out, and that's a while back. What is this important information? I'm listening. If it's to do with Senator-General Morin's mistress, don't bother, we know everything.'

'No, it's not about that. I really have to get in touch with Manuel, he's an old friend. Do you have a phone number, an address, an e-mail address, anything?'

'No, but I think I remember him heading for the Bordeaux region. He liked that part of the world.'

'Thank you, I'll keep you posted.'

I hang up and lean back in my chair, thinking hard. Vivaldi is still buzzing in my head. All those inter-cutting violins are stopping me thinking. I order a Lagavulin malt whisky to flush out the irritating noise. The waiter comes back and sets a thick heavy glass down on the table. Just the sound of it is a pleasure. As I scroll through blank pages, I pick up the cold glass and raise it to my face. I smell it, swirl the drink round and watch the teardrops of alcohol run down the inside. Peaty moorland unfurls at my feet in the mists of a fresh new day. Here and there, an occasional fire wafts a smell of grasses and ash, mingled with a sea wind heavy with spray and salt. At first I barely skim my lips over the glass, then I take a good mouthful. A strong smell of humus and earth spreads through my mouth and invades my head. The alcohol warms my soul, I can feel it sliding round my body, flowing into every last corner of my being, soothing my loneliness, healing my weariness. The subtle aroma carries me away, sharpening my senses, arresting my thoughts. I can hear the sheep bleating in the hills. I climb down the grassy mound, walking between the graves. She is sitting on the shore below me, wearing flimsy veils of cloth which afford glimpses of her body, the object of my desires. She is kissing a man, passionately, and I watch this endless kiss for a long time. I walk towards them. She looks at me and smiles, then whispers something in her lover's ear and he, too, turns to look at me. So it was him. I should have guessed. As I walk towards them I pick up a big branch, gripping it firmly. It is hard and solid. The bark has peeled away over time and the wood beneath is soft and smooth. I am completely ready now. I can hear the wind in their clothes. She is still smiling as I choose exactly where the blow will fall.

I wake with a start, one hand supporting my forehead, the other clamped around the glass. The little clock on the computer shows I have been asleep for almost two hours. The restaurant is gradually filling up with young city types, their eyes either vacant or filled with boredom. I take off my glasses and give my face a good rub. Fangiolini's number is still on the screen. I learn it by heart before asking for the mobile again. As I dial the number I wonder whether I should stay and eat here among the cool and the hip, but I decide I have been here far too long already.

The telephone rings feebly and a man picks it up almost immediately.

'Hello, Manuel Fangiolini.' His voice sounds croaky and tired, shouted down by a blaring television.

'Hello, Mr Fangiolini, I —'

'Just a minute,' he interrupts me. I can hear him getting up, and the background cacophony stops abruptly. He picks up the telephone again:

'Yes, what is it?'

'My name is Steve Harvey, from the *Chicago Herald*. I'm writing an article about the most shocking crimes of the French Riviera, and I'm interested in the Bouteille case. I know that at the time you wrote up the incident for *Nice-Matin*. Could we possibly meet to talk about it?'

There is silence on the other end of the line. I do not know whether he has rumbled me or simply doesn't know how to reply. Still dopey from my sleep, I forgot to use an American accent.

'Yes, of course,' he says eventually, 'the Bouteille case, I remember. A girl was butchered. The police van and the presumed murderers ended up at the bottom of a ravine. No survivors. That was it, wasn't it?'

'Absolutely. Could I come to see you at your home? Tomorrow afternoon, perhaps?'

He agrees to meet me and explains how to get to his house, an isolated spot in the Leyre delta known as the Arcachon Basin. He has no true address in the sense that most people would recognise, accustomed as we are to our street numbers, post codes, subdivisions labelled with As and Bs, apartment numbers and entry codes. I get up and pay before going back out into the subterranean street. Fangiolini referred to the 'murderers'. If he knows I was not alone, why did he not say so in his articles? I wander along the corridors until I find a fast-food outlet, where I take great delight in an insult to culinary art and even to human dignity itself. As I chomp on the flaccid concoction I think about the next step as rationally as I can. I need to be on the Atlantic coast at midday tomorrow, which leaves me with few options. Flying or hiring a vehicle are not open to me, because I do not have a credible form of ID. It will have to be the train again. Shame, I hate trains.

The escalator drops me back at the surface. The streets are

crowded, it is that time of the evening when people are going out, to the cinema or for a meal. I walk over towards the fountain where I left the moped. It had no anti-theft device of any kind on it, making it extremely attractive to thieves. The only thing missing was a note with the words 'STEAL ME' on it. I am intrigued to know if it will still be there. Yes, it is: just as I feared. Some good Samaritan has even moved it and put it in the parking slot for bikes. Things really have changed. I no longer belong in this world. I don't understand it any more, unless I understand it all too well. There is something unbearable about this new society: it gives off a whiff of disinfected brains.

I sit astride the machine and point it towards the Gare Saint-Lazare. My buttocks have hardly touched the seat before I see three men in the wing mirror. They have appeared from the shopping arcade and are running towards me. One of them shouts out a reverberating 'Stop!' Its echo runs round and comes back to me several times before dissolving in the hubbub of the city. I jump off the machine, lose my glasses and flee across the bustling precinct. They are faster than me, but I have a bit of a head start. I jump over a rubbish bin and cross a busy major street without even looking. Horns blow, tyres screech. A loud crump of dented metal precedes angry shouts, which are swallowed up a moment later. I am running as fast as I can, but I can hear my pursuers' footfalls not far behind. I don't know whether this weak, shapeless body will be able to do what I want of it for long. I come out facing the Pompidou Centre, taking a fraction of a second to marvel at this visionary building and its complex elegance. Suddenly, two agents in dark-blue coats appear to my right, with the firm intention of barring my way. I make a sharp turn to the left, straight along the paved square in a state of desperation. I don't understand why they haven't caught up with me yet – these are trained men. I resist the urge to look over my shoulder and just keep on running. It won't be long before I am completely out of breath. I can already feel my strength giving way. I skirt round the multicoloured pipes of the famous edifice and hurtle down a boulevard heading for the Place de la République. The footsteps are right up close now, I can hear rhythmic, athletic breathing, the counterpoint to a long supple stride. They haven't caught up with me because they don't want to: they're wearing me out, waiting until I can't go any further and they can claim me, frothing at the mouth, dripping with sweat and unable to breathe. Unless they're hoping to kill me with the exertion, when some vital organ gives up. I can't go any further, the pain is too much. Everything hurts. My heart's going to burst out of my mouth in a great stream of blood and saliva. All of a sudden I see a white Peugeot 405 bearing down on me, swerving and missing me by a hair's breadth. It ploughs up on to the pavement at full speed. I hear the dull thud of battered bodies and look round. The car has stopped. The middle of the windscreen bears a star shape splattered with bloodied hair. My two pursuers are lying on the tarmac. The first moves and tries to call for help, but doesn't utter a sound. The second is motionless, his legs twisted, broken. I stop. The doors open. Three huge Blacks get out. One of them waves me into the car. I get in. Another is holding an axe, which he brings down several times on the man who was trying to call out. Dropping the axe, he jabs a flick knife into the other man's neck with practised precision. Now I want to get out of the car, but they stop me. A fourth man, sitting on my left, puts his hand on my arm. I turn round. It's the old man from the kitchen, the one eating rice. He pats my hand reassuringly. His three companions get back in quickly, slamming their doors, and the car sets off at full pelt. Moments later we pass two police vans with screaming sirens. I try to breathe, I want to thank them, but all I can manage is a groan as I throw up.

It isn't long before the car turns left and slows down. We cruise through the Jewish quarter and stop on a traffic island: everyone gets out. They make me run a dozen metres, then jump into the back of a rusted white van. A driver is waiting for us. We set off past Bastille and take the Rue de la Roquette. We are sitting on cardboard boxes, which insulate us from the freezing cold metal. The man opposite me is cleaning his axe with a wet-wipe. I watch him, disgusted. He left his knife in the agent's neck.

Eventually, the old black man turns to talk to me. He is a scrawny, huddled figure and I catch sight of his face only intermittently as we pass under the street lights. He speaks with great composure, and his voice reminds me of the sound silver foil makes when you scrunch it up.

'You met my nephew last night, didn't you? And you came to our apartment. I saw you in the kitchen, you had some rice. But you brought the National Militia along with you, and they took everyone away. I don't think any of them will come back. No, my nephew definitely won't ever come back. They don't tend to do that any more, night raids like that. They've learned from experience. They've become much more discreet and meticulous in arresting the no-rights. They didn't call in a whole barrack room of troops just for a pathetic Mongol, which is what you look like on the outside. The National Party seems very interested in you, and we're interested in you too. Did you know there were two officers from the Political Police with the agents? I knew they were there. You see, I was hiding too. As you can imagine, they don't send that sort of outfit just to get some retard back to his care home. My nephew wasn't involved in politics. Since his father's death he's been like a son to me. I knew him better than anyone. They didn't come for him: they came for you. You're worth more than you think, but you don't know it. Do you know why the lions are after you, little gazelle? What are they planning to do with a Spirit?'

'I don't understand any of it. Who are you? Did you really have to kill those two policemen?'

'Who we are doesn't matter much to you, but you can call me Baron Saturday. All you need to know is that this State doesn't only have friends. For years now, deep in the forgotten quarters, in an underground world and in places where the agents never go, there are growing numbers of people who are trying to change things. We want to be free again, and the way we go about it is an exact mirror image of the brutality that's inflicted on us. We give as good as we get to the powers that be. It's our way of trying to show them what they are. Don't be too shocked about the fate of those two men. You have no idea what they would have done to you if they'd caught you. You would have regretted not being properly dead.'

'But I'm not...'

'Don't go trying to invent a life for yourself. I know about

Spirits, too. I know what you are. There weren't any Spirits before they came to power. I don't know what they managed to do to bring people back like this, when their time here is over. Nor do I know how to interpret the way you look, what it means. But I do think about it. By the way,' he adds, handing me the sunglasses I had left on the kitchen table, 'you'd better put these back on when we get out of the van.'

I decide not to talk to him about my investigations or the journey I plan to make. It seems sensible not to say too much about it for now. I have arranged to meet this Fangiolini and I still intend to talk to him, but I might change my mind. Why bother trying to rehabilitate myself now that I am party to the murder of two agents? I think back to the man in the wheelchair and what he said to me. I am not trying to find where I belong any more. I am trying to leave a world in which I no longer belong. There is only one thing I want: to understand and to get away, so that all this madness can end.

The old van comes to a stop in a terrible graunching of gears. The driver reverses clumsily into a parking space, bumping the neighbouring cars, then cuts the engine. We get out and scuttle some fifty metres down a narrow, ill-lit street with old white-fronted buildings on either side. We disappear under a wide porch and cross a courtyard steeped in darkness. I can feel the paving stones under my feet. I look up and see a square of starless night sky. The others walk quite easily in total darkness, while I stumble and trip several times. They pick me up every time. We go into the building and feel our way up the wooden staircase, which groans underfoot. I count the floors. We climb to the fourth, the top landing. I hear the clink of keys and glimpse a brief gleam of metal, then a door creaks. We go in, but remain in total darkness. I hear footsteps on the floorboards, curtains being drawn, a door close. Eventually, a feeble bulb glows red on the ceiling. It hangs in the middle of a sitting room full of dilapidated old cane and bamboo furniture, a straw mat on the floor. There is now only one other man – the youngest of the group – with Baron Saturday, as he calls himself. The others have disappeared. The old man sits in a wooden chair and asks for a drink. The young man opens a sideboard and takes out three cups and a terracotta bottle. He pours out a colourless acidic-smelling alcohol, then sits down. Baron Saturday invites me to do the same.

'Sit at the table for a while. Allow me to introduce Friday, my son. Drink, it will warm you up, then you can wash and have something to eat. We'll give you clean clothes too. This apartment is one of the ones we use for what we do. It'll be best not to stay outside tonight: there's going to be quite a hunt and we're the game they're after. It was complete madness going into that restaurant to do research on the net. Without a scrambler you could have been picked up so easily. You just had to type in the wrong words and that would have been the end of you in a matter of seconds. We watched the agents setting up an ambush outside. They waited for you a long time, long enough for us to be ready too. Why are they looking for you? Were you a political activist? Were you a member of an opposition party or a banned union? Were your family or friends some kind of militants? Do you have some compromising documents? Photos? Writings? Account books? Have you stolen money from them? Did you set up or perpetrate any assassinations? Were you involved in forbidden activities, like a mixed marriage or taking in foreigners?'

I shake my head slowly in reply to each of his interrogations. I tell him a bit about my old life – who we were, my wife and I. What we liked, what we did, what made us happy and sad, how sad it makes me that I have lost her. I admit I voted for the National Party during those wretched elections. He tells me there have been no more since. The young man suddenly barks a harsh insult at me in a language I don't understand. Baron Saturday tells him to be quiet and starts lecturing him. I do not know what he is saying, but I understand how bitter Friday must feel – a tall, strong, young black who had to watch the world he was about to taste go rotten before his eyes. He saw his adolescent dreams dissolve the moment he reached out for them. I look at him, but say nothing. I do not apologise. I look deep into his eyes, devouring the life dancing in his pupils. Through his eyes I can penetrate the warmth of his flesh. I can hear his heart beating, his blood flowing. I can feel the air drawn through his lungs and the slow pulse of his intestines. This started as a game, but I am beginning to enjoy it. I derive a cruel and intoxicating pleasure from carrying on. The tendons in his neck tense, his face becomes distorted with pain and the blood vessels begin to bulge. Suddenly a tear of thick dark blood springs from his eye and runs down his cheek. The old man flicks up his hand, so that I can no longer look into Friday's bleeding eyes, and my victim falls from his chair with a long groan of pain and despair. I now understand how the dogs died, and I think I have killed him, too. But I haven't: he is sitting on the floor rubbing his head and wiping his cheeks.

'The person you're so scathing about was someone else,' I tell him, 'and he's long gone. Don't be too quick to judge the person in front of you now, because I've already been judged. You're alive, you need to worry about the future. You'll have time to worry about your past soon enough.'

'Let that be a lesson to you,' the old man says, turning to Friday. 'And don't forget what he can do. If you had deigned to listen to what your uncle taught you, you wouldn't have been punished like that. Never let him look you in the eye.'

Friday stays sitting on the dark wooden floor for a while, then struggles to get to his feet before going over to the kitchen and dousing his head under the running tap. His feet are unsteady on the creaking floor. I listen to his ablutions while Baron Saturday pours another swig of eau-de-vie for a dead man. He moistens his lips with his own drink and starts to talk again:

'In my village, the elders used to tell the children stories about spirits and the dead. Their stories could be sad, happy, beautiful or joyful, they could be filled with dancing and singing, but in their own way they were also strange and terrifying, so it was difficult for us to distinguish between the real world and the imagined world. You see, my childhood was spent cradled in a spiritual life that a white like you will never experience. Later I moved here and I forgot about all that. I disowned it when it was my very essence. I abandoned a part of myself in order to forge links with other people. But I always knew that somewhere beneath our hectic city lives there were other lives, subtle discreet lives. The lives of all the people who pass among us, absorbed by their own destinies – the Spirits. And you're one of them.'

'Do you envy me?'

'No, because there is no peace in your condition. Being what you are means being alone and hunted. You are like a beast at bay, a lamb among wolves. I can help you, but I will ask you for favours in return.'

'And if I refuse?'

'You are still free for a while and that time is absolutely yours. I can't force you to do things against your will, but if you agree to help us, then I will help you too.'

This man is being devious. I suspect some plan is stewing in the depths of his old brain. Some plan involving me. I trust him no more than I trust anyone else. If he wants me to help him I will raise my price. I reel off everything that comes to mind, making it sound more like an order:

'I need false papers, a vehicle for getting about, information on anyone – police officers or journalists – who investigated the Bouteille case: their names and addresses. I want the guest list from that wedding, and I want to know what they saw, what they heard, what they ate and what they drank. Last but not least, I want to know who the girl was, this Agnès Bouteille. I want to meet her parents, her friends, to know who she saw, who she wrote to, talked to, worked with and slept with. I want to know everything. I want to know how I landed up in that van full of lunatics. And only then will I help you.'

'I doubt you've been granted enough time to achieve all that,' said Baron Saturday, 'but that's not for me to decide. For now, we can provide you with something to eat, something to wear and somewhere to sleep. My son will give you some means of transport because you said you had a long way to go before tomorrow. Right now we're going to eat.'

The old man calls Friday, who comes back out of the kitchen. He is still badly shaken. His back looks hunched under the weight of an invisible burden of fear or resentment. He opens a wooden box, takes out some plates and cutlery, and lays the table in silence. His eyes flick away every time I look at him. His father gets up, rests his hand on his shoulder and says a few words to him before leaving the sitting room. Only then does Friday turn towards me.

'Come with me,' he says, staring into space over my shoulder, 'I'll show you the garage while my father makes us something to eat.'

He goes over to the door and takes a bunch of keys hanging from the horn of a dark wooden mask. As we go out on to the landing I catch sight of Baron Saturday crossing the sitting room, a live chicken in his hand. He gives me a friendly little wave. Friday closes the door behind us. We climb down the stairs, feeling our way and trying to keep our footsteps light and silent. Then we go out into the courtyard and I follow him to what looks in the darkness like a garage door. I hear the metal clinking and the latch creaking. Friday opens the door and then closes it behind us. I wait, motionless, listening to our breathing in this hot, echoless space, unable to gauge how big it is. He lights a candle and stands it in an empty bottle. We are in an old garage which has become a dumping ground, cluttered with cardboard boxes, tins and rags. He takes a few steps and starts moving things aside. I watch him, but offer no help as he struggles with heavy packages and sheets of metal. I sit down and gaze at the wax trickling over the bottle while he works. Under all the jumble Friday eventually comes to a large shape. It is covered in a ghostly white sheet ringed with greasy marks.

'There, with this you could be anywhere tomorrow.'

He tugs the sheet, which slips to the ground revealing something that warms my heart. In the dancing orange glow of the small flame I see a motorbike half lying against the wall; a big single-cylinder all-terrain bike which looks as if it has not been used for years. The studded cross-country tyres have been replaced by wider, smoother sporty ones. A huge phallic carburettor stands out along the flanks of the machine and all that is left of the exhaust pipe is a small vestige guaranteed to wake the whole neighbourhood with its decibels. The name given to this sort of creation – which defies the laws of Nature, an improbable coupling of two opposing philosophies – is 'superbike'. A formidable machine on bumpy little roads and fiendishly efficient in towns. Just one piston, the size of an artillery shell, to make your blood boil to a simple, savage rhythm. This treasure was once beautiful and loved but, abandoned here with no owner for all these years, she has languished and wilted, her splendour faded.

'Is it yours?' I ask Friday, not taking my eyes off the lovely machine.

'No. It belonged to a friend, Big Soldier. He was a crafty bugger. A dilettante, a crook and a biker all rolled into one, and he managed to get himself registered unemployed in three different regions. In other words he lived the high life. When the National Party came to power they started sorting out the benefits and allowances given to the really poor, because they said the only people benefiting from them were the niggers and retards: all of whom became no-rights. Big Soldier was arrested and his house was sold to offset the overpayments. I don't know what happened to him, but when he was caught he was on this bike just outside where I lived. They left it on the pavement. I went and got it in the night and it hasn't moved since. That was a long time ago.'

I go over and pick it up, the keys are in the ignition and there is oil in the engine. I sit astride it and give it a shake: no swill of fuel, it must have evaporated long ago. Even the smell has gone. I turn to Friday and shake my head, pointing at the bike's empty fuel tank. He tilts his chin towards a red jerry can by the door. I put the bike on its stand, get the can and fill the tank right up to the brim. Then, before I even ask for it, Friday passes me a hand-pump and points at the tyres. I pump away. Now we can get down to serious issues: for a moment I worry about the battery, then I remember that the thing is kick-started – it's going to be quite a work-out. Ignition, choke, and let's go for the burn.

The kick-starter is a small pedal that you have to thrust with your full weight to fire up the engine. Where some people simply press a button to get their machines humming, others pull on a lawn-mower wire or employ the kick-starter, risking abrasions, hernias, strains, prolapses, slipped discs or worse. But there is something even more vicious: the kick-starter's revenge. The good people who invented this pedal did not foresee that, at the tiniest hiccup from a deranged engine, the kick-starter shoots back up with enough force to break a tibia or a fibula. So it is with a combination of determination and caution that I start pumping the little metal lever. Nothing doing. After five minutes of fruitless effort I give up, sweating and out of breath. Friday just leans against the wall, arms folded, watching me.

'She just doesn't want to know,' I say bitterly. 'The lining's rusted through or the ignition's had it. I won't be going anywhere on this. All right, just one more go then I'll give up – unless you've got the tools to take the whole thing to pieces.'

'I've got the tools. We can start with the spark plugs.'

So here I am taking out that vital organ made of metal and porcelain. It is cloudy with soot: that was a worthwhile exercise, then. I brush it up, put it back and screw it in before throwing Friday the spanner, which he catches.

'Do you think it'll work this time?' I ask.

'Have a go, you'll soon see.'

So I stand up on the foot board and bring all my weight down on the kick-starter, squeezing the accelerator at the same time. The place fills with a deep, stuttering, deafening roar, which reverberates through my chest like heavy rocks tumbling down a mountainside. The thing is alive, quivering and growling, hammering at my ear drums like a succession of cannons going off. I smile, probably for the first time in a long while. A beaming smile, as I listen to that sound, the generous, refined sound of a beautiful engine working properly.

'Okay,' says Friday, tugging at my sleeve. 'You should cut the engine or we'll be asphyxiated. Let's go up and eat now. You'll have time to play to your heart's content later on.'

I grudgingly cut the ignition, then cross the courtyard and climb back up the staircase, which I am getting to know. We talk very little as we eat the chicken, which has no seasoning except for its own greasy brown stock. Baron Saturday sits opposite me, devouring his food with a hearty appetite. I spot a few downy feathers in his hair as he chews on a bone.

'Now,' he says eventually, spluttering on his food, 'you're going to go to this meeting you've arranged, wherever it is, and when you get back we'll have gathered some of the information you've asked for. Then it'll be your turn to help us. Are you still happy with that?'

'Yes.'

'Good.'

'What else?' I ask cautiously.

'You'll find everything you need to have a wash in the bathroom, then you'd better go. It's already late. No regrets or questions?'

'No.'

'Good.'

After finishing my drumstick I get up and go off to wash. The bathroom is small, dark and dilapidated. There are wet clothes drying over the bath and green trails of lime-scale under all the taps. Through the frosted window panes the lights of the city form stars ringed with tears, and I look at them, filled with sadness that I am not somewhere else. A lukewarm shower is hardly a luxury. The tepid water streams over my skin, taking with it the green apple fragrance of the cheap shower gel I found lying around. Some clothes have been left on a chair for me: woollen socks, T-shirt, polo shirt, jeans, sweat shirt, jacket, trainers. Still no underwear: I'm too embarrassed to ask for any, so I get dressed knowing from experience that I will be cold on the journey. Then

I go back to join my hosts and tell them it is time I left, but they keep me a while longer. We drink tea, lying on silk cushions embroidered with gold thread and eating pastries that glisten with sugar. We talk and I feel good, finally soothed now that my body is sated, lulled by a calm feeling of security, which makes me want to sleep.

After quite some time and a number of inconsequential conversations, Baron Saturday hugs me to him. Friday has disappeared. The Baron tells me to go, saying the garage door will be open and that I must leave without looking back, however good and at peace I feel when I am with them. Before leaving, I ask him for some newspaper to slip under my clothes. I am beginning to feel frightened again. I do not know what lies ahead. I do not want to leave.

VI

So it is that I set off late into the night, long after the patrols have given up looking for us, carried south by the hoarse roar of the huge engine. Friday left a crash helmet for me by the door. It is too big, but it shields me from the cold and from prying eyes. I cut noisily across the sleeping town and not a soul deigns to appear. The machine jumps, twirls, bounces and belts along as the fancy takes it, utterly uncompromising and oblivious to the rules of the road. Soon the surface becomes smoother, I am past the ramps and interchanges and my route gradually straightens out. The city's street lights are far away now and I emerge from the orange glow that bathes all major urban roads. In the distance I can see the cold of utter blackness drawing nearer. The darkness of true night, the black of sleeping countryside. As I come closer, the darkness wins over the orange phosphorescence, eroding it, digesting it until it has vanished. Then comes the forest, lit by a single feeble light. I hurtle at top speed along the grey ribbon of tarmac, which twists again now, as if contorting with pain, as if the road is in agony. I can no longer hear anything, not the hammering of the engine or the wailing of the wind. Only the white lines still catch my eye, gleaming in the dark, scudding past rhythmically. They are the Braille score for a vast harmonium.

I launch myself along straight stretches and curl my way around corners, flattening myself on to the bike up hills and leaning into bends, getting a bit of an angle if I can. At times I drop a gear to accelerate all the more, at others I race through the gears so as not to lose any time. Villages explode at me along the way, gusts of houses that quickly disappear. There are long interludes of shifting woodland with their countless nocturnal scents. Heavy clouds of leaves tumble towards me, briefly illuminated by my ephemeral presence. I used to love woods, the way they rustled in the wind and snapped underfoot and mingled ochres with greens. I would have liked showing all that to my children, to my Lucy. I can see her in her little dress sitting in the fallen leaves. Where is she now? Is she playing at His right hand, sitting on clouds of leaves as I hurtle by beneath them?

I am travelling through La Puisaye with its ponds and woods. At Vierzon I get on to the A20 heading for Limoges. When I have been going for what feels like an eternity I begin to doze. This machine is not meant for motorways. I start lagging and falling asleep, swaying and swerving. I pull myself together several times until I have had enough of the fear and the angry flashing headlights, and stop at a service station to fill the machine with petrol. I park it as far as I can from the light, at the very edge of the car park where the tarmac gives way to undergrowth. I get off and walk a little way, dazed and exhausted, then stretch a few times to try to ease the stiffness in my carcass. My hands are still buzzing to the vibrations, even though they have stopped, and the din of the engine still rings in my head. It dissipates gradually, replaced by the faint but insistent whistle of silence trying its best to make room for itself. I sit at a picnic table, waiting for the swell of this internal sea to stop altogether.

Then, with my crash helmet in my hand, I walk slowly over to the brightly lit building to have a coffee. There are drivers sleeping in their cars, sales reps caught short by the night, exhausted holidaymakers, drunken partygoers. In their cabs, with their curtains drawn, lorry drivers can finally reap the rewards of their calendars. The long, modulated melody of passing cars lulls these sleeping figures. The glazed door to the shop opens with a sigh to reveal rows and rows of shelves carrying overpriced food and cheap knick-knacks. I navigate through the maze of racks and displays to get to the coffee machines. A woman in a blue overall and a green headscarf is pushing a steaming cloth over the floor, while a great hulk of a man with a moustache is reading a card as he sips his drink. I slip a few coins into the slot on the dispenser. It quivers and thrums, then delivers a strong sugary espresso. I pick it up and the machine wishes me a safe onward journey in three languages. Turning my back on it, I warm my hands on the cup. The first newspapers have not yet arrived. I buy a sandwich to pass the time, then get another cup of coffee.

Two bikers come in: tall and blond, dressed in leathers for a long journey. From the Netherlands or Germany perhaps. They give me a nod, when they see my crash helmet. I nod back, without taking my glasses off. They must think I am rude because they ignore me after that. It doesn't matter, I need to go and pee anyway. Motorway toilets are a chapel, a crypt that must be visited on every motor pilgrimage. Designed to self-clean with powerful jets of water, you could blow up a cow with dynamite inside them and it would take only a few minutes to remove every trace. The place is just a concoction of floor tiles, wall tiles and tiny pieces of mosaic in nuanced shades of white and grey-blue, intended to soothe drivers exasperated by the road, by screaming kids or by the fact that their paid holidays are over. On the right the stalls, at the end the urinals, on the left four basins and a huge mirror. I head towards the urinals, resolved to honour them with a visit. The floor is still wet, testifying to the recent labours of the woman in the headscarf. In spite of the bleach there remains the stench common to all public conveniences. When I walk past, the mirror does not deign to reflect my image at all, not even my clothes or the helmet in my hand. I wonder whether other people enjoy the privilege of seeing my reflection or whether it is lost for ever. I think about it without finding an answer, but the uncertainty does nothing to stop me peeing. I zip up my flies and wash my hands in a Pavlovian reflex to be hygienic. Someone pulls the flush behind me, I hear the door open and in the mirror I see a man coming over towards the basins. He is wearing a hat and scarf and he too is wearing dark glasses. He stops still and looks at me in the mirror. I turn towards him, intrigued. Nothing, no one, just the door to the stall slamming shut. Yet I can see him in the mirror. He comes over to the basin next to mine. The tap turns all by itself while his reflection operates it. The water starts to flow. He washes his hands. I dry mine. For a while we watch each other in the mirror.

'It's the first time you've met someone like you, isn't it?' he says, breaking the silence.

'Yes, what's going on?'

'We can't see each other except in these bloody mirrors. How long have you been back?'

'A few days, I've lost track. I was away twelve years, and they've been hunting me down every minute since I've been back. How about you?'

'A few months, I'm not really sure. I was gone for seven years.'

'Did you meet the man in the wheelchair, with his dogs, big dogs like black horses, and so thin?'

'Yes, I saw the man and his dogs. The animals tore his throat out right in front of me and he laughed while they did it. I don't know who that character is. Probably a guardian, a porter or some crazy servant. I met him in the street in a town beside a lake in Guyane, not far from the church where I died. In the early days I thought I'd survived, but I had to accept the facts. Like the fact that I don't have a reflection.'

'How did you die?' I ask him.

'My church caught fire during a service. It all happened very quickly. I saw women and children going up in flames like torches. At first I thought agents from the National Militia had bombed us with phosphorus or napalm or some other hellish concoction. The church was an important local centre for the Resistance.

I discovered recently that it was me who laid the bomb. A pyro-plastic device, which was quite new at the time. I don't know how I could have done something like that. I've no idea why either. Anyway, I managed to get as far as the transept and I thought I came out through a little basement window, the molten lead from the panes streaming down on to me. I was holding a little child by the hand. He must have been three, maybe four. The dogs took him when we got to that weird deserted town full of ferns.'

'How did you manage to get back from there?'

'I hid in a boat. Once I arrived here I just had to get used to my circumstances. The hardest thing – you'll find this – is waking up to the loneliness again every day, constantly having to accept that your loved ones have gone and the world you knew has been destroyed.'

'I've already drunk from that cup,' I say bitterly. 'How many of us are there?'

'I don't know, a handful, a few dozen, a few hundred, maybe thousands. Who knows? You're the third I've met. We can't see each other, you realise that. It means our chances of meeting are very limited... but mirrors show us to each other.'

'Why have we come back? What do we have to do to get away again? What does it all mean? What are we? Restless spirits? Ghosts? Phantoms?'

'I've no idea. Maybe whoever finds the answer to that earns the right to leave again.'

'What did the others tell you?'

'Virtually the same thing. A violent death, a deserted place, the Down's syndrome guy in the wheelchair with the dogs. Then coming back like this, and always this obsessive quest to understand the circumstances of their deaths. It's the same for you, I'm sure.'

A young man suddenly comes in, interrupting our conversation. He heads straight for the urinals at the end. We stop talking and just stand in front of our respective basins. Something is bothering me. I'm not sure what. My companion runs the water harder and carries on quietly:

'And how did it all happen with you?'

'I died in a police van which crashed, somewhere in the country around Nice. I met the man in the wheelchair at a big house in the middle of a huge garden in the mountains. I can remember hearing crying and wailing, lamentations coming from the depths. I'm frightened of hearing them again. I get the feeling my voice might join all those other sad, lost voices. The rest isn't very different from what you've told me. Do you know any way of contacting the others?'

'No. I don't think we're meant to meet each other.'   .

The young man has finished and comes over to wash his hand in the basin next to me. He takes a squirt of soap from the dispenser, then starts rubbing his hands absent-mindedly. As he is rinsing them under the tap, he looks up to smile at me in the mirror, gives a start and turns sharply round to look at us both, still with lather all over his hands. He freezes, looks in the mirror again, half opens his mouth and gives a feeble 'Wha?' Then there is a sharp thud of flesh and the poor sod falls backwards in a flurry of little bubbles. The other man punched him in the face and I can see in the mirror he is running for the door.

'Don't stay here!' he warns me before slipping through the doorway. 'Get back on the road. We may meet again somewhere else.'

The door closes behind him. I step over the guy on the floor. His split lip is bleeding over the tiles that were so spotless a moment ago. Another job for the woman in the headscarf, I think before leaving. And then, to my surprise, the service station cafeteria is groaning with people. There are a couple of dozen strong young men queuing up to buy coffee or tomato soup. They all seem to be built to the same pattern. When I notice that they are all wearing the Party colours I have the inspired idea that they must be a team for some kind of ball game; they are probably on tour. Taken aback, I stand by the door to the toilets for a moment. They are not basketball players or rugby players. More like footballers, yes, football, that must be it. One of them comes past me and pushes the door. He has hardly set foot inside before he rushes back out shouting:

'Shit, you lot, come and have a look! Mario's had his face punched in!'

He turns towards me and finally seems to register my presence. His brain cells make the connection.

'He did it!' he says, pointing at me.

His long, straight white finger points me out unwaveringly. I am guilty. Judged and condemned. I must pay the price, probably in some brutal, summary way. No forgiveness, no redemption, the people want revenge and – if possible – a bit of a show. For a moment the common sense and the level-headed calm of my previous life resurface. I flirt with the temptation to take my time and explain all this quite reasonably, but that little whiff of rose-scented Cartesianism does not last long. I change my mind and scarper like a rabbit, making the most of the shock and confusion created by the shouts coming from the toilets. I cover a good thirty metres outside before the first of my would-be persecutors launch themselves in pursuit, a clod of humans defecated on to the deserted car park by the service station. The bike is parked quite a long way away, but I have the advantage of darkness. The panting pack shouts out, with screams of anger and idiotic revenge. I jump on to the machine which was cooling peacefully in the chill of the night. Of course, it refuses to start. I pump frenetically on the kick-starter, bellowing furious prayers, while the bulk of the pack draws closer for the kill. The engine is flooded and it reeks of petrol. I carry on trying obstinately to start it. Suddenly, just as I am reconciled to my fate, the motor booms. I duck the first vengeful kick and squeeze the throttle, cutting through the team of amateur lynchers, who scatter like frightened pigeons. As I pick up speed on the slip road to the motorway, I chuckle inside my crash helmet, happy to have succeeded, happy to have escaped and to have met someone like me. I still have a long way to go, but I don't give a damn.

All the same, it isn't far before the quiet of the night and the monotony of the journey get the better of my newfound enthusiasm. I need the road to do something interesting, to twist itself into meanders and convolutions, if I am not to succumb to sleep altogether. I come off the motorway and travel through the dark valleys of Périgord, still heading west towards the sea. Just as the sky is brightening with the first signs of a new day the fog descends, thick, icy and damp. Beads of water seem to be emerging from my clothes and every other surface, like some unnatural icy sweat. The cold pale disc of the sun makes its appearance in my wing mirror. I keep on going, my mind blank.

Later in the morning I stop at a tiny service station to fill up again. The place is wedged between an arid cliff face and a steaming river. While I fill the tank, I look at the branches that hang down, ruffling the surface of the water below. An old fisherman drags his boat to the shore, climbs in and starts rowing gently. I am soaked and feeling the cold, but I do not give myself a moment's respite before setting off again.

I travel for a long time, until the first hints of pine trees and salt creep inside my helmet: the sea is not far away now. I came from it and I am going back to it. I have an appointment with the big pond, the Ocean. Dunes flit by beside the road and I think back to that fisherman putting his boat on the water. He must have woken at daybreak, leaving only a warm place next to his wife in bed, an area of sheet slowly cooling. I can imagine him in his garage getting his lines and bait ready, warming up his Citroën in the yard, and driving through the mist to the edge of the water where his boat waits for him. Then pushing the boat on to the river he knows so well, unaware of me watching him from the road. He will have a peaceful morning, drifting from the river to the banks, from the cold morning mist to the flare of his Gitane. When he hears the bells strike midday he will go home, possibly empty-handed, but that does not matter: that is not what he came for. His contentment does not depend on his catch, but on his communion with the elements, giving him the strength to forget the weight of his own flesh, until the next day.

The sun is high now. The fog has lifted. The sky glows an implacable, almost unbearable blue. My journey is coming to an end. I can feel the ocean's emphatic salty presence in everything. I know that it is there, close by now, behind the fragrant pine trees and the burning hot dunes. I pass a succession of oyster-farming ports, villages of little black houses with red roof-tiles, peopled by toothless old fishermen. They sit out in the sun in their red trousers and blue smocks, scraping oysters. There are nets drying over the road surface. I stop the bike at the end of the quay, where the road comes to a halt, put the crash helmet down and look at the sea in front of me. So huge and so calm. Its gentle breeze warms my face, which is still frozen from the morning mists. The sea is at high tide and very smooth, pocked with thousands of wooden stakes marking out something I do not understand.

Fangiolini lives along this coast, somewhere at the end of a maze of paths and brackish waterways. I hide the bike in some undergrowth, having learned my lesson with the moped. I am having trouble remembering the way. I start walking, leaving the salt marshes on my right, skirting round the basin with its drab beaches. Every now and then the path straddles a rusting old lock. The landscape bears the mark of every particle of silt and sand deposited over the centuries. Few people come as far as this: everything happens too slowly here. The cloudy water inexorably carving away at the banks and filling the ditches; constantly redesigning the shifting pockets of land fought over by reeds and gorse bushes. I walk along strange corridors edged with small gnarled oak trees filtering the sunlight, crossing several wooden bridges and using a ford to go through the dying limb of a salt-water river. On the far side of a vast meadow half flooded with water I can see a long, low wooden house with red curtains and an air of hostility. Some horses are grazing peacefully, but they move away nervously as I walk through them. There is no name on the letter box, but I know where I am. I push the garden gate open, head for the door and rap with my knuckles. A dog barks inside. I am tired and would like to sleep, but I know there is still so much to do before I can. After a while I see one of the curtains move, probably only a fraction, but enough for me to notice. At last I hear a woman's voice through the door:

'Who are you?'

I say nothing, not sure how to reply. I am a prisoner in the skin of one Steve Harvey, a journalist from the *Chicago Herald*. A ridiculous, puerile lie intended to cover a character I understand less and less. Who am I? I can no longer answer that question. I am a pathetic body sheltering what is left of the mind I once had. Even lies can no longer counter the truth that everyone can see. What was I? The child of ordinary people, a working man like so many others, toiling away in one of those little offices which was always dusty however often it was cleaned. I had a quiet childhood in an uncomplicated suburb: neither deprived nor spoiled. A child from Bagnolet with grubby shorts and grazed knees, playing football on a piece of wasteland, throwing pebbles at stray dogs and tramps. Later, an adolescent who showed a moderate amount of talent in the low-profile subjects he chose. A few girls, not many friends, a diploma in commerce obtained with no great passion. Just one lover: Albane, my beautiful, the very beautiful Albane, so gentle and reserved, but not too shy to whisper in my ear the words I loved to hear. My Albane, now far away and going grey. My sweet love, lost. Two children gone. Lucy, my little Lucy. Maybe in the end I died for lack of passion and an excess of mediocrity.

'Who's there?' the voice asks.

No one much any more, I am tempted to reply. This is a painful moment for me but, after letting my mind wander for a while, I find the energy to carry on stubbornly with my obscene lie.

'Hello, I'm Steve Harvey from the *Chicago Herald*. I've an appointment with Manuel Fangiolini.'

The door opens a crack and a very old woman scrutinises me briefly before deciding to open it fully. She is tiny, shrivelled, almost desiccated. She comes out on to the doorstep, wiping her bony hands on her apron, looks at me again, then says, 'Manuel isn't here. I'm his mother. What do you want him for?'

'I'm doing some research into unsolved crimes. I know that Mr Fangiolini did a lot of work on that sort of thing before he retired. Do you know when he'll be back?'

'I'd be surprised if he does come back.'

The old woman takes a step towards me, looks at me intently. The years and the sunlight have faded her eyes which were once blue. She reaches a frail hand towards my face. I do not move, letting her carry on. Carefully, she takes off my sunglasses. There is absolutely no expression on her face as she looks at me.

'Come in,' she says at last.

So I go in. It is a very large comfortable room. I can imagine the corridors and bedrooms beyond various doors. The furnishings are strangely dated. There is a crucifix hanging over the TV and, on the sideboard, a photograph of a Pope I do not recognise. She tells me to sit at the table, puts a glass in front of me, crosses the room and takes a ham down from a hook.

'Shortly after your telephone call yesterday, Manuel became very agitated,' she says, slicing the meat finely. 'You see, he came here for a bit of quiet after all that business, all the problems that developed from his articles about those murders. Yesterday evening he went into hiding to wait for you. Just as well, because late in the night two men in suits came: policemen, well, agents. They wanted to ask Manuel some questions. I told them he'd gone fishing at sea and wouldn't be back for a few days. They told me to let them know when he came back, or if anyone came to see him. They're looking for you, aren't they?'

'Yes.'

'Eat this, then we'll go and find Manuel.'

I eat a few slices of salty ham with buttered bread. The old woman gives me a glass of dry white wine. Perfect. She unties her apron and puts on some old rubber boots. Her skeletal legs look like two stalks planted in them. We go out and walk round the house to where a path sets off down a gentle slope between two patches of reeds. We soon come out on to a small sandy beach beside a river. There are several boats moored at dark, gnarled wooden stakes. Some of the vessels are full of dead leaves and rainwater, others have sunk and lie beneath the water, almost invisible, gradually rotting and succumbing to the seaweed. The old woman unties a little plastic boat bleached by the salt. We get in and she starts to row downstream, with the current, steering between small islands of sand.

'The river's too shallow to sail down,' she explains, 'so this boat gets us downriver to where our proper boat is moored. I'm not as strong as I once was, so I have to wait for the tide to help me up and down the waterway. You're not... let's say you're not what you seem to be, are you? Your mind is normal, whatever your appearance implies. Who are you?'

'I'm hoping your son will tell me that. Would you like me to row?'

'No.'

She has decided that I should not do any of the work, and her tone of voice implies that her determination and strength of will are still intact. She probably knows the river better than anyone. I also suspect that at her age she no longer really minds that some questions never have answers. Soon she will have an answer to all her questions, and that is probably why she is not persisting, happy to concentrate on her rowing.

From time to time, when the bottom of the boat rubs gently against the sand, I feel a pleasant quiver running up my back. The current carries us and the old woman keeps a sharp, stern eye on the waters downstream. I gradually relax and think for a moment that I might be able to sleep. Then I sense the penetrating cold of something huge watching behind my back. I turn round: the river has now become a vastness, an ocean opening up to me. A desert of water and wind, which restores my serene faith in solid things. Simple beauty does exist, I am communing with it. My eyes stray to the line between the elements. The old woman rows, boats sway. She steers us towards a wooden craft with a long narrow hull, like a stray gondola from a deserted Venice.

I never really understood anything about boats until I reached adulthood, until I was mature enough to realise at last that the experience was worth the learning. There were two of us, a couple of friends, a couple of young dogs holding a whole summer in our fists – the same fists that we brandished at the sky, cursing it for our lot in life. With school long forgotten at last, we killed time through the hottest part of the year somewhere around Pesaro on the Adriatic coast. That was where we met Paolo, who had seen a few more summers than us, and on one of those scalding afternoons he suggested we should go to sea with him, just a few days at the most. I was a child of roads and pavements. I have never liked swimming pools, let alone deep water, where God alone knows what sort of creature is watching, biding its time to seize you and drag you down where no light ever shines. I was, therefore, hardly thrilled by the suggestion, even when we grasped that the aim of the trip was to bring back an enormous quantity of dope from Serbia. Enough to keep us gliding for weeks. At the time we did not mind at all which forgotten country we got the substance from, we were stoned from morning till night anyway, like slabs of meat frying on the beach in a state of bliss and wonderment, waiting for our internal sun to set, and living in hope of the new dawn represented by the next dose.

A nice little spin at sea, man to man, nothing like it, I eventually persuaded myself. Paolo was not an amateur and certainly no fraud: two-masted, solid wood, no engine. The sea the old-fashioned way, navigating by the elements and on acid – the hard way. I remember the nights spent helming with my eyes glued to the needle of a compass, a hemisphere wavering with the swell like a miniature graduated Earth lurching unpredictably. I remember those rocky deserted coasts and the disturbing muted sound of distant gunfire, and Paolo, a huge joint in his hand, sitting at the prow dangling his legs in the water singing Lebanese nursery rhymes and regaling us with poems about the Bekaa Valley.

On the way back, after we had taken charge of the stash of weed which seemed more precious than our very lives, I remember the drifting and the navigational errors. One night there was a storm of Dantesque proportions when the angry sky made the sea boil until the air and the water were indistinguishable. I was helming, we had eaten pasta that night, by torchlight. I can still see Paolo pouring the steaming saucepan over the sieve in a great mushroom cloud of water vapour. We had drunk a couple of bottles of vodka in order to cope with the parmesan and the other two quickly descended into comas while I clung to the helm to avoid slipping in my own sick. When the storm reached its peak I was afraid I would die. I can remember wishing the boat would break up, so that it would all be over and the terrible groaning would stop. But it was not to be and — even though I took us further off course — we did not sink. Heaving among the torrents and the squalls, I suddenly thought I saw huge shapeless towers looming over us in the stark flickering lightning, frameworks of girders and cranes. We had strayed into a field of oil rigs. They wasted no time in flooding our pathetic lost little tub in a dazzling stream of light from their powerful searchlights. I crossed that forest of steel unflinchingly and fled, pursued by lights blazing from the sky. I never told my two companions what I saw that night, those harsh lights trained on us, those floating villages with their deep foundations. I never told them how alone and naked I felt at the time. All I wanted to remember of that journey were the dope and a robust lesson in seafaring: not just anyone can take the helm.

'Hey, are you listening?'

The old girl is mooring us to a stump.

'I'm not coming with you,' she says, 'the tide's about to turn and I'll have to get back. Manuel is on Bird Island, over there, behind that tchanquées hut. This is our best pinasse. It belonged to my father and one day it will go to my son Manuel.'

I do not understand a word she is saying so I spread my hands to show my confusion.

'Turn round, then,' she says with a sigh. 'Can you see those houses on stilts way over there?'

I close my eyes to mean yes.

'That boat there is called a pinasse,' she goes on. 'Take it and get on with it. You'll have the current and the wind against you, but the boat stands up well to the sea. Those houses are built on the western side of the island. From there, follow the channel that heads north. It's not high tide yet. If you miss your line, the incoming tide will set you right again. Once you're on the island Manuel will come and find you. It's bigger than it looks, but it's still tiny to anyone who knows their way around it. Don't go venturing into the oyster beds with the boat because of the cages.'

Still I say nothing.

'Stay in the channels,' she carries on, 'and don't try negotiating the stakes, you'll damage the hull.'

'Don't worry, I understand. What about you?'

'You're going to hand me the line and the bait from that box, there. Come on, wake up a bit, for goodness sake, and get a move on!'

I step awkwardly from one boat to the other. The blue and white pinasse pitches under my clumsy manoeuvring. A huge cabin with closed shutters separates the fore and the rear decks. On either side of the stern there are wooden seats, which also serve as storage boxes. I open the one she is pointing to and it spills an impressive quantity of fishing equipment at my feet. She tilts her chin at a rod and I pick it up, along with a box held shut by a thick elastic band, then hand it all over to her. She thanks me and sits back down in her boat before giving me some final instructions.

'You can get to the engine through the trap door at your feet. Will you know how to get it going?'

'Yes.'

'The helm is there. Do you know how to helm?'

'Yes.'

'I hope you'll manage. I'm not sure Manuel's expecting someone like you.'

'No one does. Thank you for your help.'

With one jab of her oar the old woman turns her boat round and starts to move away. There is a word inscribed boldly on the stern in gold capital letters. ELVIS. She is going fishing with the King. I open my mouth to say something, but she is no longer looking at me, already concentrating on lining up fish hooks on her gnarled knees.

I turn away, kneel down and open the trap door to the engine. An old single-cylinder, gleaming with grease and half drowned in sea water. I press on the little squeezer for the fuel pump, turn on the ignition by flicking a small switch and start the machine with the help of a button on a very rudimentary instrument panel. It coughs, sneezes, spits, wipes its nose and eventually fires up with a loud rattling from the track rod. The cooling water spurts out in a series of ejaculations through tiny holes in the hull, blending with splutters of diesel to form iridescent shapes on the surface of the sea. I close the trap door and let the wheezy little creature warm up.

Meanwhile I look in the cabin: there is somewhere to sleep and probably some way of preparing a meal, judging by the rows of unlabelled tins which fill the shelves. Fishing rod, boots, gaff, harpoon, buffer buoys, bailer, buoyancy aids, shrimp nets, ropes – a real boat cabin, cluttered with piles of things dirtied by years of use. I take off my shoes, because the floor is several centimetres deep in black water, and walk across carefully to avoid stepping on anything sharp. There is always some forgotten tool or jagged piece of rubbish under the water just waiting to remind you how tender your meat is. Still, I reach the prow unharmed and untie the line, which is wound round a great chunk of polystyrene weighed down with seaweed. I go along the gunwale to get back to the helm. I have no urge to go through that gloomy, flooded cabin again.

There is a pull-tab to regulate the throttle: off we go. I am amazed how briskly the boat accelerates, the elongated hull carving silently through the waves, heading west. I turn round to wave at the old woman, whose name I do not even know, but she is already too far away, almost a dot at the end of the channel. Never mind. I pull the throttle right out and point my nose into the wind, the helm clamped between my knees. The boat skims over the water. All along the way there are countless channels edged with wooden stakes forming an inextricable web of possible routes, but I stick to the widest lane, aiming straight for the two tiny buildings. As I look towards the distant shores around the bay, it feels as if I am navigating across a huge water-filled crater formed by some cosmic prehistoric cataclysm. It's an attractive idea, but there is no weighty sense of turmoil or past catastrophes here. It is a peaceful place, conjured by water and wind.

The buildings on the waterfront draw nearer and I can understand the old woman's sour tone when she mentioned them. They were probably once beautiful, but these two houses perched on tall concrete stilts are now too clean, too painted and too conspicuous not to seem artificial. I pass between them and the effect of them towering several metres above me is faintly disturbing. A staircase leads down from each building and disappears under the water. On the far side a narrow channel heads northwards, a deep furrow snaking darkly through the shallows. I nose the pinasse carefully into it, occasionally rubbing against the soft sheer sides of the tiny waterway which soon takes a right-angle turn and bears westwards into the middle of the island with its mixture of water, sand, silt and pale, stunted vegetation. The muddy eroded banks are crawling with crabs keen to scuttle out of sight. The further I go, the narrower the channel becomes, and the boat's draught eventually forces me to drop anchor. Everything falls silent again. I sit and watch. The tide is going out and the water is dropping, going back to the ocean, disappearing out to sea. Soon the boat will fall on to its hull to wait for the flow of the next incoming tide. I step out into the shallow water and climb up the slippery bank to have a look around.

The island is larger than I thought. The western coast is a long way off and seems to be covered in trees or thickets beneath which I can make out more of those black cabins used by the oyster-farmers. I start walking towards that wooded village along a little path peppered with acrid white guano. Every now and then I see a green or red cartridge, evidence of past shooting expeditions. In places hastily positioned railway sleepers bridge the gap over deep ditches, which crackle with marine life. Yet everything appears motionless, there is no one here but the birds in the sky and the crabs in their holes.

I eventually reach the village, which turns out to be just a huddle of cabins beneath the trees. I still have to cross a shallow sandy creek to get there. I step through it, carrying my shoes. At last the water is blue and the sand white. A man is walking towards me on the opposite bank. I did not see him coming, sheltered as he was from the powerful sunlight. We stand facing each other at the water's edge. He is tall with red hair and an elegant bearing, which sits oddly with his three-day stubble. He is wearing military fatigues and has turned them up to the knee. We stay there for a while, with our feet in the water, looking at each other. I eventually decide to break the silence.

'Manuel Fangiolini?'

'Yes. Would you like me to call you Mr Harvey or would you prefer a different name?'

'You can call me Steve. You certainly live in a beautiful part of the world. I envy you having all this on your doorstep.'

'Well, actually I hardly ever come here except in the autumn to shoot. It was your phone call which brought me back to this – shall we say – discreet place. I thought someone would call me eventually, because of what happened all those years ago. I knew it would catch up with me in the end. You could say you're my Beethoven's Fifth, my friend.'

He laughs, takes hold of my arm and invites me to walk along the bank with him. He gazes at the horizon for a moment before speaking again.

'You're not really a reporter, are you? You're not an agent either. But you're peculiarly interested in the Bouteille case. It was a long time ago, but I haven't forgotten the turmoil and strain it put on anyone who tried to look into it. Is this your first investigation into unsolved crimes?'

'To be honest with you, it's the first, the last and probably the only one. Why was there so much fuss about it? It was only one murder, after all.'

'Did you know Mr Bouteille, the father?'

'No. Who was he?'

'Patrick Bouteille? He was assistant to the Chief of Police in Marseilles, but he was also, apparently, a mole for the Revolutionary Castroist Party.'

'The what?'

'I know what you're thinking, but don't get hung up on the name and don't be too quick to scoff. Apparently Mr Bouteille sat in his comfortable office at the police headquarters and, for many months, gave information about agents' movements and operations to extreme left-wing terrorist groups. People said that his daughter was one of these activists, planting bombs, and that she was blackmailing her father. Do you remember when Commando Krivine took control of the first terrestrial TV channel?'

'No.'

'Shortly after they reintroduced the death penalty, a group of extremists – with close links to the Liste Communiste Revolutionnaire and glorying in the name of a dead left-wing agitator – erupted on to the set of the State news programme broadcast by the Global Network: forty million viewers, at the very least. One man punches the presenter in the face, and a young woman sits down and starts reading their manifesto to a gobsmacked nation. Meanwhile, her friends keep the studio technicians under control. The girl is Agnès Bouteille. Just after this show of strength, right in the hallway of the TV channel's building, the commando unit is decimated by the Special Forces of the Political Police. But the girl, now *she* manages to get away.'

'Well, it sounds like quite a publicity stunt, anyway. What did their manifesto say?'

'Pff. The usual drivel. Except that they were threatening to circulate documents to the Press proving that the Party was using massive doses of drugs to make the population docile, tractable. There were some who suspected as much, but this group had actually managed to get hold of documents that left the matter in no doubt. Anyway, the girl got away. The Political Police are no fools and it wasn't long before they made the connection with her father. They probably tried to get hold of her by threatening him.'

'I can't really see a father denouncing his daughter like that.'

'Nor can I. Actually, I don't know. There's a lot I don't know. I'm convinced the girl had some sort of hold over her father. None of the articles based on my investigations were cleared for publication. The few lines on the subject that appeared in *Nice-Matin* were put together by an automatic generator. You can't imagine the hysteria there was surrounding the story. You could almost touch it.'

'But she wasn't just killed,' I say. 'She was butchered, slashed. I saw her. This was more than a simple political elimination. Especially as nothing happened to her father.'

'Don't be so sure. Two weeks before she died, I gather he resigned for health reasons. He was replaced and no one ever saw him again. Nothing, vaporised. Seen like that, the whole business is pretty clear, but there's a lot that's yet to be explained. My story is just conjecture. There's nothing to disprove the hypothesis that Agnès Bouteille could have been killed by a rival cell of the Workers Movements. At the time almost all of the left-wing groups were involved in clandestine activities and had resorted to extreme violence. The agents didn't make it easy for them. Anyone who was caught was almost guaranteed to betray their little friends under torture, and it was often easier for these groups to simply remove anyone about to be caught.'

'Who got in the way of your investigations?'

'Mainly the Political Police. I've never been able to meet the detective in charge of the investigation, um, I can't remember his name…'

'Lefort. Superintendent Lefort.'

'Exactly. I spoke to him once on the telephone. He seemed

terrified, I remember now. Neither he nor any of the detectives involved wanted to talk to me. I don't know what happened to him, but I know that a young detective called Dumontet was transferred to a place called Die. He was probably too inquisitive. That's one reason why I think it's more likely to have been a political assassination, perpetrated by the Government. But be careful, if you publish that your life will be in danger, and your loved ones too. Even though this is ancient history, your enquiries might have reactivated some State network. But I get the feeling there's more to it than that. You're digging up something huge. Watch your back. I couldn't believe how quickly the agents turned up at my house after you called. I can sniff out trouble from a long way off. That's why I made myself scarce the moment it was dark.'

'I know, your mother told me.'

We carry on walking until we reach the beach to the south of the island. He crouches down and looks back out to sea. He takes a long twig and starts drawing shapes in the sand as he talks.

'There are several things I never really understood about that case. Mainly the brutality of the murder. What was the point of that hideous ritual, when a bullet through the head would have done? And then there was the accident involving the police van taking the murderers away. Killing the assassin is still the best way of keeping the people behind a murder out of trouble. That's been done before.'

'I was in the van. I saw everything.'

Fangiolini's twig snaps in his fingers. The end is dropped. He squats there in terrified silence.

'So you must be the murderer,' he eventually says anxiously, 'the one who caused the accident? You were pronounced dead. What have you been doing all these years? Where did you hide?'

I tell him my story in detail, trying not miss anything out. After a while I have to take off my glasses to prove that I am telling the truth. I can see the disgust in his face and suddenly realise just how repulsive he finds me. It makes no difference my explaining that I am someone else, that I have done nothing, that I never touched that girl, telling him there was another man there with me, who may have seen something while I knelt in the grass, waiting, horrified. I know it is no good. This Manuel Fangiolini is a journalist through and through: obscene, voyeuristic, calculating, avid for promotion and probably prepared to betray trust. He loves anything sordid and is drawn to horror for the frisson it affords him, for the glory it showers on him and for the money that readers are prepared to fork out to experience that same frisson in their turn. I have seen the disgust he felt for me. Even so, he is still speaking to me.

'You came all the way here, to this far-flung beach, to tell me this, and I only half believe it. I think you came to get information for your employers. Do you know who those Blacks really are?'

'I don't have an employer. I'm on my own. Those people helped me when I thought I'd lost everything. They're part of the Resistance, they're fighting, not to change anything but just to avoid disappearing altogether. I came here to tell you that I'm innocent, that I have this terrible secret weighing me down. When the truth is finally out in the open, then maybe I'll be free. I came so that you could give me some names, names of people who followed orders and tinkered with my pathetic life, turning it into the... the tormented existence I have now.'

'You should go and see this Dumontet. If you play him right, he might give you some information. Hard to say really.'

'Does your Dumontet still live in Die?'

'Probably. I've told you pretty much everything I know. I had some documentation at one time, the autopsy report among other things, falsified beyond belief. But all my archives were confiscated. What will you do now?'

'I don't know. I'll probably try to contact this Dumontet, then I'll go back to Paris in the hopes of finding more information. I don't know what those people are going to want in exchange.'

'One piece of advice: be careful with them.'

We stand in silence for a while. I have about ten hours to kill before the next high tide, but I do not know whether I will be able to get back in the dark. Fangiolini claims it is easy, but I feel a kind of apprehension, foreboding. Navigating at night has left its scar on me, a gaping wound splattered with bright light. We walk on along the beach for a moment, just for the pleasure of it, and watch the shadows lengthen. All of a sudden the little ditty of a mobile chirps up. I had not expected him to have one in a place like this. He raises his hand apologetically before moving a few paces away to answer. Those things are ruining our lives, alienating us by making it impossible for us ever to be alone and wholly ourselves. That is very much the case here, in this instance. It has become impossible to escape from the vast human canvas, from its constant demand for productivity and from whatever place we have been assigned within it.

I watch the tide going out. There are huge banks of silt and sand, spiked with fossilised stakes and striped with long rows of cages like lines of heavy coffins. I turn back to gauge what stage the call has got to. Fangiolini is just behind me, standing firm and square, still on the telephone. In his other hand he has a huge revolver aimed at my head. The chrome-plated weapon watches me with its single black eye. Its sides flash a fiery gold in the low-angled sunlight. Fangiolini puts the telephone slowly back into his pocket. He speaks to me one last time, looking me right in the eye.

'I'm so sorry.'

A fatal mistake. I had just taken off my sunglasses to rub my nose. So I bury his body on the beach in a deep hole which keeps filling with water. Perhaps I should not have done that. It would probably have been wiser to have asked him more questions. But once I had taken hold of his spirit I did not dare relax my grip, in case he found the strength to pull the trigger. So I sucked him dry, to death. He collapsed on to the sand fairly quickly, his eyes still open, but I carried on to the bitter end, until his heart stopped beating. I do not feel bad about it. I am curiously exempt from any feeling of remorse. I admit I have never wondered whether I would be able to kill someone. I never even wanted anyone dead, but I killed him, and it has no effect on me. I would have thought I would be distraught, screaming and shouting on the beach, but no: nothing.

I pick up his gun — an incredibly beautiful, heavy thing — and look at it for a while, sensing the power distilled in it. Then I throw it as far as I can out to sea. Next I find the mobile and scrutinise that in turn. There is probably a function which displays the number of the last person to call. I prod a few buttons for a moment, but soon accept that I will not get anywhere with it. The mobile joins the gun in the world of silence.

It is late. I am tired and I really should sleep before leaving. What was that mysterious telephone call Fangiolini received? Was it really Fangiolini? What was he doing here? Why the change of heart? What did they whisper in his ear? More questions without answers – but I am getting used to that. At least I have a name and a place: Dumontet in Die.

I go back to the boat before it's completely dark. It is lying patiently on the damp sand. I take a few tins of food, a camp stove, some matches and some rudimentary cutlery, then I sit in the stubby vegetation and warm up a tin of sausages in white beans. The little blue flames glow feebly but give no real light. I am glad of this because I do not know how long Fangiolini's mysterious callers will wait before coming to look for me. I can imagine them sniffing me out already, noses to the wind. They probably realise that their plan has failed. They won't wait long. I hope the tide comes in soon so that I can get away from them. I still need some time to get to Die and talk to this man. Maybe he will know more about it than all the others put together. I eat off a metal plate, leaving alight the little crown of blue flames to keep me company. Each one is perfectly motionless, its smooth contours clearly defined. They are burning but look frozen, like the flames that crown the Fallen Angel on his dark throne.

I walk slowly across the heath, dragging the girl's body by the foot. She can join the other one on the pyre I have built for them: a great heap of dried grasses, strong-smelling peat and reeds thrown up by the sea. I shattered their skulls, both of them. It couldn't have happened any other way. She leaves a long trail of reddened sand behind her. I do not know how it came to this. I suppose I could not bear the betrayal. It hardly matters now. I throw her dislocated body on to his. Now that her soul has flown she seems to weigh nothing. I look at them again for a while, naked on top of each other one last time. It is too much for me: I light the fire and sit close by where I can be intoxicated by the smells of burning grass and grilled meat. Thick white smoke lifts up through the air, a huge slow-moving tower. An opaque plume folding in on itself, unfolding, rising and eventually dissolving high up in the air where the wind never drops. Before me the quivering orangey glow of the young fire feebly lights the pale column of smoke. But soon the flames are ardent, roaring, driving the darkness right back. The huge blaze rears up, shakes its fiery mane and snorts a whole galaxy of golden sparks, sowing the sky with living stars. I lie down with my hands behind my head. It will be a long night and a magnificent show.

The biting cold wakes me. I fell asleep still sitting with the plate of food on my lap. The stove has gone out, probably used up the gas. I finish the cold congealed beans in their greasy sauce and stand up stiffly. It is late in the night now, the constellations already look old. Orion is rising, warning it will soon be autumn. I take a few steps towards the boat and find that it is afloat and the creek has filled with water. The clicking sounds of crabs out hunting reach me from the banks. I swallow, abandon my makeshift camp as it is and climb aboard. The boat feels familiar now and I get back out to deeper water without much difficulty.

Fangiolini was right about that, but it would not have saved him. In order to be sure I'm headed the right way I take the time to stand up on the roof of the cabin to scan the horizon. Every coast looks identical, dotted with little beads of white and orange light. In the end I head for the closest, towards Arcachon, which looks all too brightly illuminated from here. I avoid the town centre and travel diagonally towards the first dark area to the east. After a long half hour at sea, the pinasse runs aground in the salt marshes.

I jump down, disappearing up to my midriff in the silt. For a moment I think I will never heave myself out of the heavy cloying mud dragging me into the depths. After considerable struggling and contortions I do manage to tear my way out and crawl up to the road which runs along a bank some way ahead. It cuts across the huge area of marshland on a heaped bed of chunky hardcore which I climb, still dripping with muddy water. It must be very late, there is not a single car on what seems to be a big main road. Everything is silent and deserted. I decide I should head cautiously for the town, taking cover in the tall grasses if need be.

I now have two options: go back to Paris or go straight to Die. After walking a few hundred metres I decide to give my hosts in the capital a bit more time and to try my chances in the Alps, on the other side of the world. It is strange to see just how many of life's necessities you can lose when Fate really puts its mind to it. I do not know how to carry on with my journey. No chance of getting the bike back because – even though I know more or less where I left it – I have no idea where I am. A small sign saying 'AIRFIELD' pops up along the way. I stand and think for a moment at the foot of the metal post. I suppose I could divert a little holiday flight, complete with pilot, and get it to fly there. What sort of range does a plane like that have? I do not know. How could I threaten a pilot to get him to do what I want? Would he be able to get across France from west to east just like that, without maps or guidance? Perhaps a well-sharpened razor would do the trick. I briefly regret getting rid of Fangiolini's monstrous gun. That is exactly the sort of thing I would need to be master of the skies. I eventually decide that, for now at least, I should give up on the idea of an aeroplane – far too risky. I carry on along the road as the night draws to an end.

I walk in darkness for some time without seeing anyone at all. The road is completely abandoned. As I skirt round a tall bush I come to an abrupt stop and look into the distance. I can see the black water and the island I have come from. Helicopters are flying over the sea. I cannot hear them, but I can see them peering through the darkness with their powerful searchlights. I know what they're looking for. The predators are out hunting once more. They hover and dance and cut across each other in their distant silence, caressing the ground with brushstrokes of light. I carry on walking, watching those sinister fireflies. The tide carried me away long before they arrived. They may be good at this, but the elements are on my side.

The first houses soon begin to appear, precursors of the town ahead. Dawn slowly illuminates the world around me. I can feel the light swelling behind me and I step into the town hand in hand with the day. The place still looks summery, though it is late in the season. Swings hang motionless and swimming pools are covered this early in the morning. I walk along a wide avenue lined with low-slung white villas. There is no one about. The sun finally peeps above the horizon: I do not turn round, but the warmth on my shoulders comforts me, like a pat on the back from a long lost friend. Now that the sun is up, I can have a good look at myself. I am coated in dried grey sludge, like a man who has just emerged from the ground, a child of the earth, a statue of clay. I try to get the worst of it off, but soon give up. I am hungry again, and stop outside a baker's which is just opening. I go in, earn a scornful glance and come out with a croissant in my hand. I am going to walk into the centre of town to find the post office: Dumontet, Die. That should be enough to get a useable address, a new goal, a reason to carry on.

I head for the fishing port. The sun is climbing in the sky and the smell of the sea growing stronger, spreading, penetrating everything and imprinting itself on me. A stench hits me, a stink of sludge and diesel, of wet rope and forgotten lobster pots, of cooling engines and sardines being unloaded. The street lights have not yet gone out when I walk past the huge covered market where trawlers empty out their catches almost before they are moored. Polystyrene boxes, wooden, metal or cardboard crates, plastic cages, pots, creels and lines; white shells and gleaming fish. The auction room overflows with noisy bustle and plentiful catches, a streaming, stinking place. This is the High Mass of the sea, celebrated by bearded priests in yellow oilskins and blue boots. The pink building opens wide on to the narrow quay overlooking the huge port. I walk between these sturdy men, occasionally stepping aside to let them pass. For a moment I feel as if I have already dreamt of this place but had trouble remembering it. And so I continue on my way among the men rushing to buy and those in a hurry to sell. I pass those who are setting off and meet those coming back, then I leave.

As I cross a large parking area full of white lorries I find a curved piece of metal on the ground. I bend over and pick it up. It is probably some piece of fishing equipment, a big metal hook with a round wooden handle. I hold it in my hand, look at it, turn it over a couple of times, slash it through the air, just to see, to know. A man standing in the opening at the back of a refrigerated lorry is watching me and does not look altogether comfortable. I stare at him for a moment, then slip the hook into my belt.

To save a bit of time I cut across the beach, a long thin strip of sand hemmed in between houses and boats. Ever since the port was built, the flotsam tirelessly brought back by the sea has been piling up here to suffer the final stages of disintegration. I walk carefully between old planks of wood spiked with nails, car tyres, bottles, plastic bags and tin cans, all crystallised by the salt and the sun. It is a dismal place and I can imagine what life must have been like for the people who lived in these seaside houses before the sea wall was built around the port, a wall which now means they have to live with their feet in the mire. At the far end of this sordid accumulation of detritus I climb back up on to the quay and look at the rows of moored boats. I am sure I have dreamt of this place, and the memory is still vivid. I do not really know what these dreams I have at night mean. Everything in them is so like what I see now, by the light of day. Further on I drop back down on to the beach, a real beach this time, the sort where the sea carries off almost everything it brings in. Even so there is a huge yellow digger shovelling up long strips of kelp, stranded there to be dealt with by the locals. The huge machine empties its scoops of seaweed into dump trucks parked close by. The local authorities are going to some lengths to make the beach pleasant for tourists, the same ones who will spend their money on car parks and parking fines to give their melanomas time to germinate in the fiery glare of a sun turned unwitting assassin.

I stop to have a quick clean-up under the showers on the beach, taking off my clothes and washing naked, facing out to sea. The beach is deserted or nearly, and the nearly can hardly help being taken aback. I clean my clothes thoroughly. The dried mud comes away in clumps or crumbles into dust carried off by the breeze. I get dressed again and carry on heading towards the town centre. I am almost presentable, although far from overdoing it. A little further on I step off the sand and make for the main shopping street, Arcachon's beating heart. As I walk past the hideous casino I find it difficult to believe that this place was once beautiful, a seaside town with big brightly coloured houses, intricate wrought-iron balconies and long wooden verandas facing the sun and the sea. The success of mindless tourism has unleashed a tsunami of vulgarity on its rather dated elegance. Anything beautiful has been carried away, and silt has been deposited everywhere: seafront architecture, urban buildings, road pavings, shop windows, knick-knacks, jewellery.

Arcachon's main post office is almost as well signposted as the station in Nice, but it is not open yet. I spot a wooden bench and sit down to wait. The sun is climbing in the sky. Eventually a sleepy-looking post office official comes to unlock the heavy, glazed doors. I enter a huge concourse bathed in sunlight, which streams on to the white marble floor through tall arched windows. I head for the computers provided for customer enquiries. This seems to be a free, unlimited service – which is almost suspect – so I go about looking for my Dumontet in Die quite openly. No results, probably precisely because I haven't paid, I tell myself. I widen the search to neighbouring towns, then neighbouring areas. The implacable machine now produces quite a long list of names, with variant spellings. I sort through them, constantly looking backwards and forwards between the screen and the big map of France on the wall. I draw up a list of Mr Dumontets, in order of how close they are to Die, making a careful note of each address and telephone number.

Then I go out and buy myself a phone card from a little shop opposite: there is a line of kiosks nearby, standing in the glare of the sun, and I head towards them. When I get inside I think hell itself could not be more stifling. I start systematically telephoning my way through the list, inflicting the same speech on each everyone who answers, sometimes a labourer, occasionally a craftsman, mostly of no interest. Nothing which smacks of a policeman prematurely put out to pasture. After a dozen or so attempts I start running out of patience, without actually losing hope. I work my way through a succession of responses: surprised, incredulous, stupid and suspicious. At last I come to the call I was hoping for. The man lives a long way from Die, a very long way in fact. He is one of those whose names I almost did not note down.

'Mr Dumontet?'

'Who's speaking?'

'Hello, I'm Steve Harvey from the *Chicago Herald*. I'm doing an inquiry into unsolved crimes on the French Riviera. My next article is about the Bouteille case. I've had a long interview with Manuel Fangiolini, who mentioned you. Would you like to comment on this case which, I know, caused you quite a lot of trouble?'

There is a silence, a long one. I know in that first second that I have hit home. It is him. He is hesitating, panicking, doubting, asking himself a hundred questions. Perhaps my call is just a trap, perhaps I am offering him an opportunity to get it all off his chest and settle the score. He weighs up what he could lose against what he might gain. I wait. The silence seems to last an eternity. Perhaps he was convinced he had been forgotten for ever. Even among the dead there are only a few who are that lucky. At last he makes up his mind.

'I need to think about this. Give me your name again, and tell me how I can get hold of you.'

It is my turn to be wary. He is a policeman. I know he will use the time to find out about me, and he will of course discover that there is neither a *Chicago Herald* nor a Steve Harvey. That will hardly win his trust, and he will then probably refuse to speak to me, hiding away on his mountain top, suspecting some sort of trap set by the vengeful authorities. I decide to pre-empt this and to blow his mind with revelations.

'Okay, listen. It doesn't really matter what my real name is. I've decided to get right to the truth of that girl's murder. I've got some very hot information about the case. The deal is simple: either you take the risk of speaking to me and you get your revenge on the people who sent you off to your mountain pastures, or you stay in hiding waiting for the Political Police to come knocking at the door. I'm putting a hell of a lot of pressure on them at the moment. I've decided to stir up the shit, do you see what I mean? My life doesn't really matter, I'm dead anyway. As for Manuel Fangiolini, he was murdered yesterday, just after he told me about you. I don't have any time to lose. It's your call.'

Dumontet seems to excel in the art of silence. Even though it is impossibly irritating, I decide to give him a chance, and I wait. After a long while, by which time there are fat drops of sweat running into my eyes, he finally answers.

'Right, okay. I live at Lus-la-Croix-Haute, at the Jarjatte to be precise. It's in the Drôme region. It's not hard to find. There's only one road and I live at the end of it, in a thatched house. If you try anything on, I'll take you down. Get it?'

'I've got it. I'll be there tomorrow. You won't regret this.'

I hang up and leave, streaming with sweat and completely sealed – in the culinary sense of the word. I lean against the cabin to regroup my thoughts, then go over to the fountain to cool off my face. This is another reminder that the weak body I have has precious little endurance. I sit down to catch my breath. Who would have guessed it could get so hot in that glass box.

The railway station is very close by. I walk across a tree-lined car park with its orderly rows of cars and buses. When I am about thirty metres from the entrance to the shabby building, I take a couple of steps to the side and hide behind a plane tree. The agents are here, I can smell them. They are on the concourse and on the platforms, waiting patiently for me. I can imagine their shadowy crouching figures. Taking the train was not a good idea and I cannot contemplate another journey by bike, having barely recovered from the previous one. My arms and legs feel pummelled, my back broken. My hands are riddled with blisters and, to be honest, I am desperately short of sleep.

So I set off in the opposite direction, trying to walk like someone with nothing to be ashamed of. Even if I do not look casual, I imagine I look like nobody important. That suits me fine. Passers-by seem idly indifferent. Every day I feel as if the people around me are slightly more distant and superficial. Before I finally leave I had hoped I might be able to see the people who were dear to me, to tell them the things which could not be said before. How disillusioning: no one waited for me, and who even remembers me now?

A few blocks of houses further on I come to a bustling street lined with market stalls. It is market day, a day of abundance. A dense crowd moves slowly along the heaped displays of food. Each individual has his or her own goal and yet as a whole they seem animated by some well-ordered movement, a slow convection like a human soup simmering on the hob. Pyramids of apples and spit-roasted chickens are taken away in plastic carriers, baskets and shopping bags. Not a single customer is carrying a crate or pulling a trolley. Little canvas shoes and limp berets, flowery housecoats and support tights. Groups of old people talk about last week's weather while they wait to see what next week's will be like. There is some bickering, a few exclamations, some discussion. Fishmongers scale, butchers slice, market gardeners peel, and they all harangue the crowd, singing the praises of their wares. Around me I can hear the sound of coins clinking and changing hands. The noise of it all is making my head spin, the bustle making me feel faint. Again I have to run away, abandoning the market with its seething activity and heading down a quiet road into a deserted part of town. I stop for a moment and stand motionless in the middle of the road, before carrying on aimlessly.

At the end of a cul-de-sac lined with houses with brightly coloured shutters I see a fragile cream-coloured 2CV. I come to a decision: I will make her mine. A quick glance round reassures me that we are alone. I come closer to her, being careful not to make too much noise. I don't want to startle the girl as I circle her slowly. The thin bodywork flows in long curves punctuated with globes. I stroke one rounded headlight, pat the wings and flit my fingers over the bonnet. Then I unhitch the hood and slowly roll it back along the roof. Next I grip the top of the door to ease it down softly but firmly, creating a gap so that I can climb in. I settle myself gently on to the front seat. Her suspension groans when I lie under the dashboard to inspect her intimate depths. It is not long before I have found the button I am interested in, and I begin my deft manipulations, which prove more delicate than I had anticipated. I have to start again several times before I get what I want. At last, without any warning (or precious little), the lovely thing starts to quiver and treats me to the sound of her youthful voice. The small two-cylinder engine coos like a turtledove. I put her into first gear and set off. I need a cigarette.

VII

THE ART OF DRIVING IS entirely encapsulated in handling this
2CV. Rarely has any car required so much care and attention, so
much nimble fingering and circumspection, on pain of murderous rebuffs and treacherous kicks. Double-declutching, nifty
footwork, the relationship develops with many pitfalls. I gather
speed along the quiet street and turn into a huge boulevard
barred with useless speed bumps for which I do not even have to
touch the brake pedal. The Citroën bounces along limply even
when the road surface is smooth. I leave Arcachon with my foot
to the floor, and head for Grenoble. Through the wide curve of
the interchange on to the motorway, the little car leans on her
suspension, pressing me up against the window. I still do not slow
down, and I launch us into the morning sun doing more than 110
kilometres per hour. For now, I am happy just going east. I will

have plenty of time to work out exactly where he lives after Limoges.

I drive all day, avoiding major motorways and larger towns, stopping only in minute service stations to fill up with petrol, have a bite to eat and pump the tyres. At nightfall the foothills of the Massif Central appear, an arid landscape weary of its own existence. I get lost, and soon there are no more signposts or crossroads along the way. I settle for carrying on up this narrow road, snaking over the flanks of rounded mountains. The grass is becoming scarce, I leave the living world behind, and soon have to stop by the side of the road to pull the hood back over. I set off again with the heating on. It is very cold. Sterile black stones have accumulated in great cones of scree at the foot of gloomy slopes.

Sleep catches up with me just as dusk is drawing to a close. I have absolutely no idea where I am now. I seem to have reached the top of some pass that has not been signposted. I park the car on a huge clearing by the side of the road and get out to walk over to the edge. Far behind me the sun has sunk into the sea for the night. All that is left of it is a memory of warmth and some hazy clouds of red mist. Below me the bottom of the valleys look black and depressing. There are no trees, no plants, no snow, and not the least sign of life except for this road with no name. The naked stone all around me is deeply scored with undulating parallel ridges, vestiges of the ocean on whose floor these mountains were born. The rock still has the abyssal colour of those depths.

I get back in the car and lock the doors, then wrap myself in the seat cover from the front seat. I sit quite motionless, with my eyes open in complete darkness, alert but blind. Later in the night it starts to rain. I listen to the water lashing on the hood for a long time. I am still not asleep, but I am patient: sleep will come in the end.

The fire has burned itself out and the last embers have stopped smoking. I watched them go out one by one, like eyes closing. The furious flames danced all night for me, rising up to the sky in angry gusts, then falling back ferociously to consume the body left to their mercy. I watched the fire for days, not eating or drinking. Where the huge blaze once was there is now a bleak dome of warm grey ash and, peeping out of it, half buried, is her skull, cleaned of all flesh. I go over and pick it up. It is still warm. The lower jaw has fallen off, probably lost somewhere in her lover's remains. I sit back down and turn the thing over in my hands for some time. I recognise her teeth. They remind me of her mouth and her kisses. Will I ever see her again the way she was that first evening at the bar? The skull in my hand is now completely cold and so light. I drop it. It rolls and shatters at the foot of a rock. That is the end of that.

In the morning the stony world of the night before has disappeared. All I can see through the windows is an opaque grey mist, so dense that the front of the bonnet looks indistinct. I get out and walk a little way to have a pee, but not too far from the car for fear of losing it. I have slept, perhaps for a long time, probably deeply. I dreamt too, but I know that not a single car came along this road all night. Nothing ever comes here. I decide to move on again straight away, to escape the milky dawn of this godforsaken place. If I stay here, if I give up now, I will become some drifting shadow, a powerless empty ghost. I pull myself together, get in the car and slam the door. It is not over yet.

I twist the leads together and start the car. The sound of the engine hauls me back to reality. I set off, driving carefully, because, through the scrolling mist, I can sense the sheer drop at the side of the road. Eventually, after a long and difficult succession of sharp bends, I come out below the clouds, at last in a real world. The Massif Central is behind me, and life begins again along the road. Fencing makes an appearance once more, alongside electric cables, road signs and sometimes even other cars.

I fill the car up at a particularly sordid and dilapidated garage on the outskirts of an insignificant village. An old pump attendant comes over. He is filthy and he stinks. He seems to be still drunk from the day before, or perhaps already from this morning, and he lurches towards me, gripping the nozzle of the pump. He slumps against the car, a Gitane in his mouth, and as he serves me he clears his throat slowly, carefully preparing for a huge gob of spit. I buy a packet of plain biscuits and a bottle of water from his tiny shop. I move on, leaving him to his pointless, squalid existence. The biscuits are stale. My patience and understanding wear away a little more every day, and I feel increasingly diluted by everything around me. I used to feel simple contempt for human beings, now it is becoming hatred. Perhaps I should have sprayed him with the petrol he sold me, just to see, just to see his expression when I took the lighter out of my pocket. Or perhaps I could have torn his throat out with a vicious swipe of that metal hook. But, no, none of that happened, I decided to leave with my car.

We are cutting across the grim Rhône valley. I am drowsy. Everything is flat. The little beauty is driving all on her own. At around midday the mountains finally come back to me, a great wide film set, barring the horizon with dazzling peaks so perfect they look artificial. I pass Grenoble and, without realising it, let the Alps close in around me. The mountains gradually encroach on the road: it becomes narrow, steep and sinuous, going backwards and forwards, passing the same place – or nearly – with each turn, gathering height one metre at a time. Still I drive on, and on. My beauty is struggling: with every bend in the road I can feel the burning hot engine balking a little more. All around me the sheer peaks rear up from the depths of the valleys, charging at the sky and spreading out across it in a lacework of snow. The old car labours up the gradient, still a long way from those eternally white heights which watch us with confidence and disdain. Climbing up and up, following the signs. Here and there a single post indicates the altitude, which is soon very high. Then, just as a smell of hot oil starts to infiltrate the interior, the road dives into a narrow gorge which carves through the mountain. I find the darkness in this gully oppressive. A foaming torrent tumbles along the very bottom, and the gorge opens out on to a massive glacial cirque with a flat, wooded floor, surrounded by high walls of carved naked rock. Here my route follows the surging river through endless meadows dotted with flowers and edged with dark conifers. The stone walls which frame the road on either side are soon succeeded by hedges of wild boxwood, through which I catch occasional glimpses of the icy waters bouncing off the rocks below.

Thick black smoke starts billowing out of the bonnet, followed by a spurt of scalding oil, which sprays over the windscreen. The glass breaks in two with a dull crack. The engine stops without a hiccup or a whine, with no shriek of torn metal or graunch of connecting rods. It cuts out, as if I have simply switched off the ignition. The 2CV trundles on and I try my best to bring it to a halt on the verge, misjudging it and knocking into the wall. I am not hurt and get out to have a look at the car. There are strange feeble spitting noises, rather like frying, coming from under the bonnet. I look at the poor thing, breathing her last beside the mountain torrent, a little salmon come to die close to the source where it was born: the only thing it has managed to lay is a great pool of oil.

I do not know exactly what the time is, probably early afternoon. The sky can boast a good clear sun, which warms the air and my skin. Not long before I broke down I am sure I saw a sign which said 'La Jarjatte' was 8 kilometres away, but I cannot remember how far I have driven since seeing it. I take the seat cover right off and roll up this makeshift blanket: I do not know what the night has in store for me, but I have not come all this way to freeze to death. Anticipating the possibility of some unpleasant encounters, I also take the metal hook from the glove compartment. I stroke it, unable to explain the fascination it exercises over me. Eventually, I tear my eyes away from it and look up at the massive walls of sandstone, limestone and marl, before setting off to walk the last few kilometres.

For a while the narrow road remains hemmed in between the cliff and the ravine, then it crosses over a tall, arched stone bridge and is again released on the grassy meadows. I walk on. Here and there along the way there are huge anthills like haystacks of busy teeming black insects. I skirt round these domes of pine needles, their surface shimmering with well-filled abdomens. Wherever I look the long wooded slopes grow from hillocks to escarpments and eventually to sheer peaks of sharp rock. I stop to drink from a deep pool of water that reflects no hint of sky, then cut across an unfathomable chasm spanned by a broad bridge. Here the road follows the river bed where now, in late summer, only a narrow brook is running. I bend over and pick up a pale polished pebble. It feels soft and warm in my hand, like my lover's skull in my dreams.

Eventually I come to what I imagine is the end of the road. There are a few low-slung houses, which already seem to be stooping under the weight of the snows to come. Their walls are made of flat stones borrowed from the mountains; their roofs of slates carved from the rock or thatch reaped from the meadows. I walk between the houses along a path of beaten earth and I pass the entrance to a deep dark sheepfold. I can hear the terrified sheep inside barging each other in their efforts to get away. The acidic, animal heat of them catches at my throat. In the middle of the village, not far from the fountain, there is an old chapel with one black bell. I stop and look at it. I feel uncomfortable and my head is spinning, probably because of the heat or the fact that the water I drank was too cold.

The roar of a chainsaw tears me away from my nausea and uneasiness. It seems to be coming from a large building on the out-skirts of the village. There is a house with a straw-thatched roof standing tall in the white light of the sun. A man is working between two piles of wood, bent over the screaming metal of his machine. He is cutting up logs and piling them meticulously in preparation for the cold of winter. He is wearing a shirt with large red and black checks, jeans and thick leather boots. He has not seen me, absorbed as he is in his cloud of shavings, smoke and noise. I move closer. He suddenly notices me and stands up, though not abruptly. He holds his machine in one hand and stands squarely, taking his time to look me over. Flakes of sawdust flutter down around us. I feel uneasy. What would I do if he suddenly felt like a change of material? He looks strong, has tanned skin and a sharp eye, and I am so tired at the moment. I could never put up a fight against this mountain surfer. He stops scrutinising me and switches off the machine. A weighty silence settles over us. He takes off his goggles and gloves before coming over to me, nudging his garden gate aside with his knee. We stand facing each other on the road. I am the first to speak:

'Dumontet?'

'Yes.'

'Were you expecting me?'

'Yes.'

'Here I am.'

He tells me his first name is Patrick, and invites me into his house. It is dark inside, with low ceilings, everything is in wood and stone. A huge tree stump dominates the middle of the room, serving as a low table. The television is in one corner on a large flat piece of stone. Along a wall is a wood-burning stove patiently waiting for the winter when it can make itself useful. He takes two glasses from a glass-fronted cupboard and pours some syrupy white wine. Through a half-open door I can see a desk cluttered with papers, which softly reflect the colours of a screensaver. I decide to throw a bit of small talk at him.

'I had a very long journey getting here. The car didn't make it. It broke down a few kilometres back, just before the first bridge. I left it on the verge, but I shouldn't think it can be repaired. I'm not going to waste your time. You must have worked out that I've never set foot in the editorial office of a newspaper, thank God. I'm trying to find information about the Bouteille case. That's why I'm here. It's very important to me.'

'I know.'

'You investigated the case, didn't you? What did you find that was so terrible it has you ending your days as a shepherd in this backwater?'

'You're the man who was in the police van that crashed, aren't you?'

'Yes.'

'Could you take your sunglasses off, please?'

I do as he asks. The inside of the house is still dark, even without the shaded lenses. He looks at me. I avoid looking him in the eye, but I can see he is having trouble disguising his emotions. He gets up and walks over to the telephone, giving me a little wave to tell me not to worry. Then he dials a number, waits a few seconds and speaks.

'It's Dumontet. You should come.'

I cannot hear the voice on the other end of the line.

'It would be easier if you just came and saw.'

He hangs up and turns back to me.

'The pride of the Political Police will already be on their way,' he says, 'escorted by four or five units of agents. It won't be long before they turn up here. We don't have much time. My instincts were right. They've never let me down, actually, and I guessed what you were before you'd even finished your first sentence on the phone. I would never have thought that one day I'd be able to meet one of you freely like this. What do you know about Agnès Bouteille's assassination?'

'What Manuel Fangiolini told me.'

'Is he dead?'

'Yes.'

'It was inevitable, I suppose. What did he say?'

'Her father was assistant to the Chief of Police in Marseilles. She was a member of a group of extreme left-wing activists and he was telling them what various agents were up to. She was apparently blackmailing him, probably to get this information. When the Political Police made the connection between father and daughter, they were both eliminated. What I can't bear is that I was there when that young girl was executed. I saw her, dead, hanging from a tree, with her skull cracked open. They wanted me to carry the can.'

He crosses the room and pours himself another glass of wine, his back to me. The silence is heavy, palpable.

'You killed the Bouteille girl,' he says in a hoarse whisper. 'You tortured her to death. You mutilated her, then killed her.'

I say nothing, I cannot believe what he is saying. He seems so sure of himself. Looking confident — that is the true secret of success.

'You killed the girl,' he goes on, guessing that I do not believe a word he says. 'You can be sure of that. Do you have any idea how many cameras filmed you while you disembowelled her? I'll show you the videos later, and the pictures, and you will recognise your-self, trust me.'

I can find nothing to say in reply. What if he's telling the truth? Is that why that night is so confused and unclear? I try, just for a moment, to imagine myself as an assassin, as that disgusting butcher who — I will soon see — may well bear my face. My face as it was before, before I became nothing.

I am startled by a knock at the door. Dumontet puts down his glass.

'That will be Father Arnaud.'

He gets up and lets the priest in, a lean man with snow-white hair and a jet-black cassock. Before cutting across the village this man of the cloth donned a thick red down-filled anorak, which he now automatically hangs by the door. He seems to feel complete-ly at home here and heads towards the sideboard, not taking his eyes off me for a moment. He pours a glass of wine, without even looking at the bottle he has picked up. Everyone seems to drink: they must have outlawed every other vice. I find it difficult being with a man of the church. It's like an embryonic pain, the promise of a migraine or a foretaste of terrible discomfort. The priest sits on the arm of my chair, right next to me. He strokes my cheek. It burns and makes me sit up with a start. Dumontet is still over by the door.

'This is the man I told you about, Father,' he says. 'He arrived earlier. Another one. I think this one was conditioned after Wolf left.'

'Really? Now that's interesting. A Party assassin, a ghost, a sort of residue.'

Father Arnaud brings his face right up to mine. His voice is gentle. He puts his hand on my shoulder. I feel disgusted, nauseated by his touch.

'Are you alone?' he whispers.

'Yes.'

'Are you afraid?'

'Yes.'

'The fear will soon take over completely, and you'll lose all control. Has Patrick explained to you what you are?'

'No.'

'It's a bit of a long story, but you need to know. Then we can see what you might be able to do about your soul. Do you want something to eat?'

'Yes.'

'Pour yourself another glass. I'll get some food.'

The priest goes off to the kitchen. Dumontet starts speaking, leaning against the sideboard with his glass in his hand.

'Long before the National Party came to power, Omni Cartel Pharma launched an ambitious programme researching psychostimulants. They're chemicals which are thought to modulate cerebral activity, making individuals receptive to intuitive learning.'

He goes out of the room and into the study next door. I sit alone for a few minutes, hear the metallic sound of a cupboard being opened, then the rustle of papers. Father Arnaud reappears carrying a large cheese wrapped in a damp cloth. He cuts several slices from it and I eat. He stays by my side, a little too well-meaning to be truly sincere. He speaks to me very softly.

'It's always a great privilege to have contact with people like you who have come back. You are so discreet and so wary. You don't have to be frightened any more, the resurrected Christ will walk beside you now.'

Dumontet comes back from his office. He is leafing through the contents of an orange folder bulging with documents and takes out a few pages to show to me. I see symbols, dashes and signs linked into chemical patterns, they may well be meaningful to him, but they look strange to me.

'Two of my inspectors died because they read this document,' he says, brandishing a report several pages long. 'They were colleagues, friends who worked with me at the time. These reports evaluate the psychotropic properties of these famous psychostimulants. The tests Omni Cartel Pharma ran on rats showed that the drugs had a narcotic effect, but the most startling were the first trials on dogs. I think those poor scientists really frightened themselves.'

He puts the document in my lap. There is a paragraph covered in yellow highlighter. I read through it and feel sickeningly lightheaded. Hardly surprising they frightened themselves. Those poor sods had discovered the atomic bomb. I am perplexed. If what I have read is true then, yes, I raped Agnès Bouteille. I beat her, pulled her apart, cut her up and emptied her out. Yes, I hung her from a tree and raped her again, in among the guts and the blood. Dumontet takes the stapled pages back and puts them away carefully.

'What you've just read,' he goes on, 'deals with the first trials on animals. They improved their formula over a period of about ten years, when they started running tests on human subjects. Look at these pictures. Can you spot the difference between before and after? It goes without saying that the whole project was shrouded in silence, especially after they'd tested it on the man in the picture. It was so secret that at first they didn't even give it a name. A project with no name. Everyone knew what it was about, but no one mentioned it explicitly. In spite of all these precautions, however, their discovery was far too significant not to attract envious gazes or to cause the odd indiscretion. The Secret Service, with their machiavellian insistence, eventually managed to get their hands on a small quantity of the molecules the scientists were developing. Some said that Michel Palotet, the Director of Research, sold his files to the Government. At the time, those servants of the State were like a bunch of choirboys gaping in awe at what their grandfathers in the colonies could do. Nothing very serious. Still, Palotet was found beside a pond in the middle of a forest, having put a couple of bullets through his own head. Pff. Seen it all before, you could say. But the Secret Service chemists worked for another eight years. They kept on modifying the substances and the ways they could be used, adding barbiturates, benzodiazepines, neuroleptics and antidepressants, as the fancy took them. They had access to a huge pharmacopoeia. I've got piles and piles of the stuff in my cupboards. Various tricyclic compounds gave the best results, old formulae that they'd previously stopped developing because of undesirable side effects. But combined with the rest, their potential for military application was a complete revelation. I know this from a colonel who worked at the Fridge. I've forgotten his name. They used these combinations to get the foreign agents they caught to speak. The results were remarkable. But I think the product was actually too difficult to manipulate to stay in the clutches of those half-wits in berets. It was at that point in my enquiry that things started getting pretty dangerous for me. The National Party won the election and there's no question that things changed radically after that. They were such difficult times. Their victory was so insecure that they probably used the substance on a very large scale – in the water, the air or maybe in mass-market food, something like McDonald's fries. I wouldn't know. What I do know is that there was a wide variety of chemicals and that they produced a range of behavioural subtleties once the subject had been given adequate conditioning. They called that "maturation" or "instinctive apprenticeship". That was when the man in the street became calm, docile, and no one had the strength to think for themselves any more. It didn't happen overnight and a lot of people resisted it, but with hindsight the effect was striking. I don't know what route they used to get so many people maturated.'

'Where do I fit in all this?'

'A pawn. You did their dirty work for them. That's one of the ways they operate: they choose some poor sap, administer the required treatment for the relevant dosage, let him maturate for a while, then let him loose to get on with the designated task. They're rarely disappointed with the results – just ask the Bouteille girl. As soon as the assassin's done his job, the police pick him up and quietly make him disappear.'

'Is that what the Bouteille girl and her little anarchist friends had found out?'

'Probably: so there were the beginnings of an inquiry. But the people working on the case very soon started falling like flies, and I decided to escape with my wife. They really had pretty much perfected their techniques for mass impregnation, you won't be able to prove me wrong on that. It was a real struggle getting away when we were being drugged into lethargy and submission. When I think back to it now, I wish I'd made the break much sooner.'

Dumontet pauses, absorbed in his thoughts. His face darkens and the whole room seems to darken with it. He pulls himself together sharply and carries on.

'That was when I got to know Father Arnaud, who had just met someone like you, someone who looked like they had Down's syndrome, but had an unusually good grasp of the situation. We talked a lot over a long period and the information we each had matched up and brought us here, where we eventually decided to stay. We're the only two people here. There used to be a little ski resort in the village, but it's been shut down. No one comes here any more. We appear to be protected from their chemicals down in this valley. Maybe it's because of the altitude, or because we don't drink their water, and we're completely self-sufficient for food.'

He looks at Father Arnaud and stops talking. He would like the other man to take over now. The priest understands this and gets up.

'Come with me,' he says, 'we're going for a walk.'

So we go outside and wander along the little street towards the chapel. I find it difficult having him too close to me – more so here than in the house. Dumontet has stayed indoors, saying that he is going to get the pictures ready and that I will have quite a shock. The group of houses is built on a promontory above the mouth of the valley and from where we are we can see the narrow gully that the road slips through. I can even see the Citroën with the pulverised engine, a motionless dot in the distance.

'He seems very well-versed in the chemical side of all this,' I say. 'How come?'

'His wife was a pharmacist. She decoded most of the documents he managed to get his hands on.'

'Where is she?'

'She's dead. They killed her not long before we got away. It was someone like you who took care of her elimination. Patrick was in hiding when the man broke into their house. When he got home in the morning he found her. She was eight months pregnant at the time. I don't know how he coped with it. He pulled through, with my help, and the help of Christ.'

'Who's governing this country?'

'No one really knows. We think it's some sort of politico-industrial cartel, which grew out of a collaboration between the National Party Governors who were still alive and the technical directors who had set up the impregnation and maturation. Can you begin to imagine the productivity gains they would get from applying the right maturation to the workforce? Have you opened a newspaper and grasped just how lobotomised we've become? Do you know about the racial policies that now operate? The new work laws? And the ones about freedom of speech in public? Or even in private? Have you heard of the Ministry for Religions? Do you know what it would cost me to be seen in this cassock?

They've won. They've got everything. I even wonder whether they've ended up impregnating themselves and dissolving into the masses. It's such a long time since they've been seen in public that we don't even know who to challenge. We'd have the most pitiful resources, anyway.'

'But what did other countries think about these changes?'

'I don't know. No one's allowed to leave. No one wants to leave. No one can cross the demarcation lines they've set up. Every individual has a zone in which they can circulate freely. It's assigned according to their job. They just can't cross the imaginary barriers imposed by the maturation.'

'Is there an antidote to these products?'

'Not that we know of.'

'What was different about my impregnation?'

'Different products, different doses.'

'Is there some way of cancelling or minimising their effects?'

'Don't count on it too much. You're way beyond the reach of simple pharmacology. You're dead. You do know that…'

'I worked that out some time ago.'

'I'm a man of faith, so I believe in eternal life and the salvation of the soul. There are thousands of people who believe in reincarnation. Were you a believer before?'

'Not at all.'

'There was one thing they didn't anticipate. It's a bit… awkward to explain. A few years after they started making assassins, you started to appear – these strange, wandering, tortured individuals – all the same and like you, with no reflection, unable to see each other and with a special power to take life. We were in the throes of a campaign to cleanse the whole species and at first people thought that families were just getting rid of their Down's syndrome relatives who'd become a burden. There were lots of you, but you weren't easy to find, because you knew how to melt into a crowd and hide your differences. Still, some were caught. Dumontet can explain it better than me. He was involved in some of the interrogations. Then, when it was clear that you had this power, they started a big campaign of experimentation. Some were tortured, some given brain surgery, others suffered live autopsies, were burned, drowned or frozen. I've seen the films. Dumontet had access to the digital archives. I've seen it all. At first my faith was shattered, and for a while I thought I would have to give up my spiritual responsibilities. But my belief came back, stronger than ever. Do you realise that you've returned from the dead? They didn't just drug the population. It goes much further than that. They modified the human make-up, do you understand? Do you get it? You're a sign that we are sent by the Lord.'

I do not reply. He makes me feel like smiling. I met his Lord in a drab little shed where he gave me a tin of cat food to eat, before ending up as dog food himself. So here I am, a ghost in a world of zombies. Even so, there are endless questions milling round my head. What did I come back for? How long will I have to stay here? Why did he say that in the end the fear would 'take over completely'? Where will I go next? I cannot bring myself to ask him any more questions. Later maybe.

We carry on walking and arrive outside the chapel. Beside the building there is a cemetery full of tall grass offering glimpses of moss-covered gravestones, their names worn away. I stand there petrified, empty, frozen, clinging to him and burning my hand with this contact.

'I can't go there,' I manage to whisper.

'I know. It was just to see. You're damned, it's as simple as that. So you can't step on consecrated land. But the Special Forces don't know that. On the other hand, once they realised they were dealing with ghosts they really did crap their pants, if you'll forgive the expression. Special units of elite forces were set up and the racial selection campaign intensified.'

We take a few steps back and sit down on a stone wall. I appreciate the warmth of the sun as much as I do the distance between myself and the cemetery. I remember that first evening, that iron staircase leading down into the whispers and weeping. I felt the same revulsion then as I do now. We sit in silence for a few minutes and then make our way back. Dumontet is waiting for us. I make it clear that I am none too keen to watch the video files. I am not interested in them. I will take his word for it. He seems disappointed, but does not insist. Perhaps he is remembering his wife, coming across her in the early hours, turned inside out like a glove with her innards and their unborn child exposed for all to see. I still have the fisherman's hook in my belt, under my shirt. They do not know that. There is no knowing when I might need it.

'Now I've got something to show you,' Dumontet says. 'Will you come with me? We're going up into the mountains.'

As we leave I ask for a coat. They give me a warm heavy one. The sun is starting to sink towards the west. Father Arnaud does not come with us, saying he would rather get back to his cottage opposite the chapel. Shortly before leaving us he looks at his watch.

'Don't be too long,' he tells Dumontet, 'they'll be here soon.'

'I don't think they'll be here before nightfall. It'll take them longer than usual because of the mountains.'

'I'm not so sure of that.'

We walk out of the little village in silence and cut across a fenced meadow dotted with flowers. After a short time I see the extraordinary intersection of the beams, pulleys and cables of an old chairlift looming from behind a clump of pine trees. A small chalet with broken windows, probably the old ticket office, stands watch over the obsolete contraption. Rust runs along the grey posts, the metal rods are twisted and the electric wire lies on the ground. A thick cable heads off up the mountain, punctuated by the evenly spaced chairs. The gap that was once cut through the trees is beginning to heal over from lack of upkeep, and in places young pines have already reached the heavy thread of steel.

I walk behind Dumontet who, to my considerable surprise, takes a bunch of keys from his pocket and opens a large metal sarcophagus. Inside it is a small generator in the final stages of mummification. He flicks a few switches and turns the key to start the machine's engine. It obliges without too much fuss.

'It's an old electric chairlift,' he says. 'We sometimes use it to get up to the escarpment over there. I tried – and failed – to adapt our old tractor engine to the ski-tow, but in the end I had to settle for this makeshift solution. The generator's nothing like powerful enough for this machine, which needs a lot of current. So we'll be going up pretty slowly, but it's better than going on foot. Unfortunately we've hardly any diesel left.'

He picks up two heavy electric cables with large clips, one black, one red, and fixes them on to the metallic ends sticking out of the porcelain contacts. A loud crack wakes the peaceful forest with a start and scatters the birds. Dumontet is showered with blue sparks and he leaps back, his hands over his eyes. The clips are in position. Nothing happens for a few seconds, but then, very slowly and with a searing screech of seized-up axles and corroded grooves, the chairlift begins to move. I am surprised: I never thought it would still work. The big electric motor labours at half speed with a deep rumbling that the cable faithfully transmits to the line of pylons. Each metal pillar picks up the melody in its own key, depending on how far away it is, how tall and how badly corroded. The whole forest seems to be singing now. I listen. Dumontet turns towards me and smiles. I wonder what it is he wants to show me up there, but I am not worried. Mind you, perhaps I should be.

I let one of the ice-cold metal seats lift me off my feet and carry me towards the limestone peaks ahead. I do not feel like talking. Neither does Dumontet. So I let the song of the cables and the twittering of the pulleys lull me. We rise slowly up above the trees, the rocks and the torrents, edging imperceptibly closer to the huge vertical rock face, an impregnable wall round the valley. After a while we pass the last of the trees and carry on our trundling journey above bald grass. Dumontet tells me that if you look carefully at the huge cliff you can see the vestiges of age-old valleys that have been filled in and laid bare by massive telluric forces. For a long time I look at the areas he points out, as if seeing Atlantis resuscitated, until the chairlift finally deposits us at the top of the last fold in the highest meadow. We get off and he stops the engine to save fuel. The climb seems to have taken a long

time: an hour, maybe two. We are standing at the foot of a cyclopean wall set ablaze by the sun. Along the saw-edge of its crest
four steely needles of rock pierce the sky like defiant swords challenging creation itself. We turn away from this spectacular sight
and start to walk, heading down to our left along an indistinct
path which cuts across the slope. The chill grips me abruptly as
we step into the shadow of the mountain. I pull my coat around
me.

'It's cold here, isn't it?' says Dumontet. 'I like this place. It's
unusual: the sub-soil never thaws out, even in the middle of the
hottest summer days. Permafrost. Can you see the frozen water-
falls along the cliffs there? The tallest of them must be 800 metres
high. I'd like you to see them closer up. Come with me.'

We walk towards the most impressive of the frozen columns,
picking our way through fallen rocks on the hard, treacherous
ground. Any sign of a path has disappeared, replaced by hefty
stones, some of which roll away to reveal the layer of ice which
holds this part of the valley permanently imprisoned. We are very
close. I look up at last. The waterfall reveals itself to me now in all
its enormity, reducing me to the status of a microbe. Eventually I
reach the base of the white tower which drips in every direction
with the drumming sound of heavy winter rain.

Dumontet has stayed some thirty metres back. He stopped
without my realising it, leaving me to go on alone. I do not know
what I am doing at the foot of this vast edifice. In spite of the insistent icy rain, which is beginning to seep through my clothes,
I reach out my hand to touch the translucent wall. I lay my bare
fingers on it carefully, but no image is reflected back. In the first

few moments of touching it nothing happens. Then, obscurely, I hear those sorrowful murmurings again, the lamentations of the crowds of lost souls, and perhaps also long wails of infinite despair. There must be something here. Perhaps in the ice, behind it or beneath it. There is no obvious cave, opening, tunnel or gap. The weeping comes from every direction. I turn towards Dumontet.

'Can you hear those voices?' I call to him, but my own voice sounds faint and distant. 'What can you see? Can you see them?'

He waves me back over towards him. I am relieved to move away from the motionless waterfall. When I reach him I turn round and it is then that I notice that there is no torrent or trickle of water flowing from the base. Dumontet pre-empts my question.

'Odd, isn't it? The waterfall is moving slowly down the mountain like a glacier on the névé, but there isn't any water flowing towards the valley. Did you hear voices? What were they?'

'Wailing from beyond the grave.'

'Come on, let's walk back into the sunlight. It's unbearably cold here. Then you can explain what you heard.'

He is right. We are creating clouds of vapour as we speak. We retrace our steps and soon emerge into the sunlight. Only then does the aching and sadness in me become bearable again. We stop to talk on an outcrop of rock, sitting side by side and looking down into the valley. It is my turn to make a pre-emptive strike.

'When I met the man in the wheelchair, in that house, there was a staircase that led to the cellar. I didn't look down into the opening, but I heard the same lamentations coming from it and the same endless sound of dripping water.'

'You know,' he said, 'I saw some very ugly things when we started really studying your kind. I spent a lot of time watching tapes of vivisection and interrogations. They would put a thick blindfold or a hood over your eyes to protect us from your powers. The same incomprehensible, delirious ramblings cropped up again and again, the same stereotypical memories of past lives. But also stories of redemption, which I only understood much later. It wasn't easy interpreting what we heard, because after a while you were all reduced to loathing and violence. One of the creatures we interrogated told me about this place here. He told me that some of you come here and that you're never seen again. At first it sounded a bit whimsical to me, especially knowing that your kind can't see each other. Later, I started taking an interest in what he'd said. I came here, to this very outcrop of rock. That was long before I settled in the village with Father Arnaud. I saw them. I saw people like you, walking through the woods towards that wall of ice, wandering through the bracken and struggling through the snow. Sooner or later your kind come here, and they may travel to other places too. I don't know what it means, but I know that none of them ever comes back. What else can you tell me about it?'

'There's definitely something here. Something that frightens me. It was in that mansion too. I felt the same revulsion.'

'So why do you all come here? I'm convinced there's a gateway to another world. I was hoping you'd be able to go through it and leave. How come the others could, but you can't? Isn't there somewhere you feel drawn to?'

'No, not really. Until now I've been trying to find out who killed that poor girl. That was what motivated me. Now I have got my answer I'll probably go back to Paris. I know some people there. They've been kind to me and I owe them a favour.'

'And then?'

'Perhaps this place will call me one day. But not today. The ice didn't want me any more than I wanted it. I don't know how all this is going to end or what will happen to me.'

He has no answer to this. No doubt he thinks that that is our lot, for me and all my kind. The two of us stay there, staring blankly ahead. This whole corner of the huge cirque was once a ski resort, and from our privileged vantage point I can see several dilapidated ski lifts surrounded by pistes carved through the dense woods. A question niggles me.

'How did you come to realise that you were dealing with dead people?'

'The most unwatchable video files were never numbered. They were distinguished by a series of vertical or horizontal bars or various signs. In among the very worst there's one that I wanted to show you, but you didn't want to watch. It's filmed with a camera on the ceiling. It's in a little medico-legal operating theatre – all white china and stainless steel. There's no soundtrack. The poor beast is held down with metal straps, which was common practice. A technician comes in and starts reading measurements on various monitors. His overalls are the same colour as the walls, so most of the time you can only see his hands and his face. He peers at some dials, looks amazed, walks round them, checks the connections, unplugs them, plugs them back in, swaps them over. His equipment obviously can't find anything to measure. He's clearly piqued and plants himself in front of the man and they talk briefly. At the time no one knew about the power you have, so the poor man doesn't take any precautions and gets taken. He freezes, shakes, foams at the mouth, is sick and has convulsions. You can see his mouth distorted with pain, screaming something. Then two men in asbestos suits come in with flame-throwers, and they fill the place with boiling streams of fire. The Party must have had some inkling already and wanted to avoid possible contagion. I don't know. The camera stopped filming at that point because of the heat.'

I say nothing, so he goes on.

'There's more. There's worse. You must listen very —'

A loud wet plop interrupts his sentence. I have been showered with a warm liquid. I jump to my feet and turn towards him. Half his head has disappeared, replaced by a gory void where little jets of blood dance rhythmically. He stays sitting there with his hands on his knees then slumps forwards slowly, falls and rolls down the mountainside for about ten metres. A stone shatters by my feet. I jump aside and run down the slope towards the sparse trees below. I trip several times, slipping, breaking my fall with a hand, swaying and twirling my arms in the mortal hail that seems to have come from nowhere. I can see the bullets landing ahead of me and hear them behind me. I ply my way through the tall grass, reach the trees, and launch myself into the woods without slowing down. The machine-gun fire stops, probably because it no longer has a good sight line. I run to the deepest part of the densest thicket, scratching myself on branches and trunks, and end up falling to my knees in a large muddy puddle.

I stay there, waiting. Then I hear the echo of a distant bell ringing in the valley. The bell at the chapel: Father Arnaud's vain attempt to warn us. It does not last long anyway, the ringing is cut short, probably for want of a ringer. I cool my face from a little thread of water running between two stones, and crawl over to the edge of the woods. A pylon from a button lift lies close by, worn down by the passage of time. I do not know what equipment they have at their disposal this time, but I make an initial decision to wait until nightfall before coming out. Then I remember their amplified searchlights and infrared goggles. I am pretty sure it will be even easier for them to track me by night when the heat of my body will shine bright in the frozen forest. As I set off again I think of Dumontet: what a shame for him, going through so much, managing to hide for so long, and ending it all in a terrible case of mistaken identity. The priest will have suffered the same fate.

I crawl from trees to thickets, from overhangs to ditches, and listen anxiously to the muffled thrum of helicopters scouring the mountainside. Every now and then one of them whirls overhead, skimming the tops of the trees with a thundering of blades and rotors. I flatten myself under the lowest branches of the pine trees, where it is almost completely dark. Soon the sun will drop behind the mountains and the cold will descend – I am afraid of it. I need to find shelter quickly if I am not to die of cold. I also need some means of transport, but the village must have been surrounded and the 2CV will have been taken off to the lab. I don't remember Dumontet mentioning any form of transport, apart from the tractor. Never mind. I'll go on foot if I have to. It's not far to the village. And I'm hungry.

Along the way I look at my fingers in the dimming light. I clearly remember being splattered with Dumontet's brain, yet there is no visible trace of blood on my hands or even my clothes. I cannot see why. I should logically bear the stigmata of his execution, but no: nothing. Another thing I do not see is the agent who comes out from behind a huge black rock without looking. He knocks into me quite violently and for a fraction of a second we stand facing each other, speechless. He is young, probably not yet twenty, and is wearing large night-vision goggles which look slightly phosphorescent in the half light. They mean I can't see his eyes. But the main focus of my attention is the massive grey machine-gun slung across his shoulder: stocky, heavy and loaded to the gunnels with lead. He reacts, swinging it round sharply to blow my head off with a burst of fire, but he isn't quick enough. The fisherman's hook punctures his chest through the plexus with one horribly abrupt upward lunge. I drive it in deeply to pierce his heart, and haul the metal hook up through his ribcage. Hot blood flows over my hand. I hear his sternum breaking, and I think I can feel the wooden handle reverberating to the last beats of the organ dying within him. I didn't want this. It just happened. We were in the same place at the same time, and his family would probably rather he hadn't been here. I hold him upright, clasped to me, putting the finishing touches to this magnificent assassination.

After laying him on the ground I hover for a moment, wondering whether I should take the hook back or steal his gun. While I hesitate I eat the chocolate bar he had in his pocket. I hear his earpiece crackle. Someone must be talking to him. They must be looking for him. I am in no doubt they will find him, but I would like to be alone with him a little longer. I drink from his flask – given that I can't drink to his health – and look at his handsome face. I, too, would have preferred it if we had never met. And there I was, thinking I envied everyone else on the planet. Perhaps everything that is happening to me isn't that bad. When I finally decide it is time for us to part company, twilight has tinged the mountains with mournful colours and the cold is beginning to insinuate itself between the trees.

I set off towards the valley again, cautiously crossing a huge treeless esplanade. I come to a clearing, probably the point where several ski runs once coverged. In the middle there is a large pylon carrying a horizontal wheel. Driven by some fortuitous force in the air, the huge metal disc is revolving slowly, occasionally emitting a feeble creaking sound, which is swallowed up by the surrounding silence. The mountains, the air, the forest: nothing is moving, but still it revolves. I walk underneath and look up to watch its wide spokes sweeping across a sky gently filling with stars. For a moment the wheel seems to stand still and the whole sky appears to spin around that motionless astrolabe.

I go back down towards the village, flitting from hedge to thicket, from copse to undergrowth, crawling through meadows of closed flowers where dewy droplets will soon form and later freeze like sequins. The first slate roofs appear, gleaming black in the night. I hide behind a wide tree trunk and spot the men patrolling and chatting. The cold is torturing me. My fingers are numb. I know it would be impossible to spend the night outside. I need shelter. I move towards the nearest building, which has a familiar smell: it is the sheepfold. I climb in through a narrow window. The sheep barge into each other, jostling and bleating feebly, but they soon accept me and let me share their warmth. I huddle in a corner and cover myself in soiled straw. During the night the sheep come and lie down against me. I sleep with my face buried in oily wool and dried droppings.

I am back on the heath. I walk for a while, and sit when I am tired. The sun is high, the heat overwhelming. I do not know where to go. I left my lover's remains for the sea to take care of. Everything is just salt and sand now. In front of me a dried shrub dances in the quivering wind. It shivers, blurry and ethereal, then − as I stand watching − it catches light between its reptilian limbs, writhing on the sand. I can see that shattered skull again, the flesh burning and the thorns eaten away by flames. There is just one eye now, in the blazing zenith, piercing through the flesh and seeing right into me.

In the morning I am reborn again on the warm straw between those thick walls: the Wise Men have not come. I lie there for a while, surrounded by inquisitive muzzles, then I leave, opening the gate for the sheep, which scatter among the houses. The roads are deserted. The agents have left. I find it odd that they never try just that bit harder, that they always seem to miss me by so little. I am delighted they do. Knowing that I will not be able to enter the priest's house, I go to Dumontet's. The door is wide open and the place has been turned upside down. His office is completely empty: they have taken the cupboards, the desk, the chair, all the computer equipment, even the ashtrays. The rest of the house is no better. There is almost nothing left. Every piece of furniture has been emptied, the beds overturned and anything that put up any resistance has been broken. I pick up a chair and have a bite to eat and drink. Then I go out and look round the outbuildings. There is no car, but I find an old bicycle, a vague assemblage of rusty tubes and pock-marked chrome. Having no alternative, I decide to use it. I find a can of blackish oil lying around, and use it to lubricate anything that can be lubricated. I pump up the tyres and check over various cogs. The thing is coming back to life. Everything seems to work, except for the brakes which have seized, and I give up trying to repair them. Will I get all the way to Paris on a bike? Probably not. I will get to the bottom of the mountain at the very best.

So it is on a bicycle that I leave that strange liminal village, the last staging post before a crossing which I may one day make. I freewheel down between the sheep engrossed in their grazing. The 2CV has vanished. The people looking for me make everything vanish in my wake. Even the pool of oil has been cleaned away. I do not know what will happen to La Jarjatte now that it has been robbed of its last two inhabitants. The houses will fall into disrepair like the ski resort, and the valley will be forgotten for ever. I do not know if I'll be able to come here again one day. I doubt it.

VIII

AT FIRST EVERYTHING GOES WELL, until the incline flirts with the 20 per cent mark, then this descent without brakes becomes a battle for survival. The least straight stretch of road sucks me down and I dice with death on every corner. I brake with my feet when I can, but most of the time I have to veer off into the grass or grit in order to slow down. I take several heavy falls, deserving to break my neck each time. Somehow I survive. At one point I really think I am going to die when I lose control of the thing through a hairpin bend and somersault over the parapet, which overlooks a bottomless precipice. By some miracle the bike and I land back on the road below, buckled and bruised respectively. I sit there watching the wheel still spinning with a little clicking sound. I take a deep breath and get back on the saddle. The bike has taken a hell of a beating, but it still works, only now it has a lurching rhythm.

We set off and the whole problem starts again, until the incline eventually grows shallower and the corners not so sharp. After freewheeling for some time I come into a small town that I do not think I came through on my way. I did not notice a sign on the outskirts and have no idea where I am. A few shops, an old wash house, a flowery square, the war memorial. I spot a bistro opposite the sandy strip where the locals play Boules. There are several big motorbikes parked in a row. I stop and look at these anachronistic machines with their taut lines and aggressive colours. I do not recognise the models, which no doubt look beautiful to modern sensibilities, but are too strange and innovatory for my outdated tastes. A huge old-style Hayabuza dominates the sleeker Italian machines with their rows of headlights and insect-like design. In those days Japanese engineers wondered what exactly would happen to a motorbike at more than 300 kilometres an hour, so they designed this sort of machine, just to see. Bikes that were as cumbersome to handle when switched off as they were powerful and honed to perfection in action. And of course they were made available to children who had just passed their test, the better to entertain the gravediggers who soon ran out of places to dig. The conclusion of the trials was that above 300 kilometres an hour you tended to travel into the next world. And with that the trend died out. Shame.

I lean the bicycle against a tree and sit down at the terrace near the bikes. The bikers are having a drink at a nearby table. They are laughing, talking loudly, showing off and challenging each other. They are also drinking a lot. They must be telling each other how many times the gates of hell have opened wide before them, how often they have narrowly escaped death. I could tell them a thing or two on the subject, but would they even stop to listen to me?

I order a glass of beer and think things through. I do not have enough money to buy one of their bikes, and I would not have the nerve to suggest hiring one. I have a few hundred euros left from old Emile – in other words nothing compared to the value of that gorgeous machine. Hayabuza, the name dances round my head. I want it. I was right to take the fisherman's hook back.

There are some old boys playing Boules. I watch them squabbling over a point, assuming indignant poses as they display their bad sportsmanship. I order another beer. Some of the bikers leave, others arrive. The beautiful monster stays. The old boys carry on playing. I decide not to count how many beers I have, happy just to watch them coming to my table.

At last the bike moves. I look up, my eyes swimming from the alcohol, and see a girl moulded into a gleaming leather jacket. A little brunette with delicate limbs, arching her back on that enormous machine. I reach out and touch her arm. She turns her back to me, freezing but not startled.

'Do you know why they called it Hayabuza?' I ask her.

'Because when you ride one of these you feel as if you're swooping down on every corner like a falcon on its prey.'

'Something like that. Aren't you afraid you'll kill yourself?'

'No.'

'Or be horribly injured?'

'No.'

She stops for a moment, apparently lost in thought, then speaks.

'I'm just making the most of it while the god of motorbikes grants me mercy.'

She falls silent again. She is a little slip of a woman with a wilful chin and a steely eye. She looks me up and down with a twist of what could be contempt on her lips. Her expression is hard to read. She seems to switch from knowing everything I'm thinking to not even seeing me a moment later. She throws her gloves on to the table.

'Buy me a beer.'

I wave to the waiter to bring us another round. She looks at me again. Her eyes are black and hard, her nose aquiline. Just as a dog and its master end up looking oddly alike, she has ended up looking like her motorbike. She seems to size me up before speaking.

'You a biker too?' she asks in a soft voice, deeper than most women's. 'I don't think I've ever seen you round here. You don't look like a local. It's just there hasn't been a population influx in these mountains for centuries, so everyone can't help looking like everyone else.'

'But you don't, your face is hardly ordinary.'

'I don't know, you could be right,' she says. 'I've broken all my mirrors.'

'Why?'

'It's a long story.'

'I don't have much time,' I tell her, but she says nothing, looking fragile all of a sudden. Still, it is no easier holding her gaze. I can tell that she doesn't know what to say, and I dare not hope that she finds me attractive in any way. It seems too improbable.

What does she think I am behind my dark glasses? She makes as if to speak several times. I see her lips moving.

'What are you doing here?' she asks eventually. 'You look like a hunted animal, covered in blood and wearing rags. The bistro manager has already called the agents and, in case you haven't realised, there's no one else on the terrace now. But you didn't notice anything, you just sat there waiting for the right moment to strike up a conversation with me. Am I your next victim?'

She may be beautiful, but she is not stupid, unlike me. I have to concede that it was absolutely suicidal to come and have a drink here, where everyone knows everyone else. I am covered in blood, though quite incapable of seeing it myself.

'I've only killed when I've had to,' I say, deciding it is safer to be honest. 'Mind you, recently I've found it easier than I would have imagined. In spite of the way I look, which I'm prepared to believe is frightening, you're the one who asked me for a beer and came and sat at my table. I probably look pretty pathetic, but I haven't always been like this. I sometimes find it difficult to know what I actually look like now. Either way, if the agents are on their way I'd better disappear. But you see, I really need to clean up a bit. Could you hide me for a while?'

'I don't think we met by chance. We should see this as a sign, as fate, a hidden meaning.'

'You haven't answered any of my questions.'

'We can't stay here.'

She gets up and goes over to start the bike. I leave some money on the table and join her beside the beast, which is growling quietly. She puts on her crash helmet and gloves and climbs on to the machine, waving to me to get on. The bike has no wing mirrors or number plates. I climb on behind and put my arms around her, just firmly enough to avoid being ejected as she sets off. I close my eyes and let myself be taken. I am the sort of person who cannot bear being driven, so I prefer not to see anything and just try to endure dicing with death. When we arrive she brakes so abruptly that my body presses hard against her, harder than I have ever held any girl. The engine stops and the bike makes little clicking noises.

I open my eyes: we are in a hotel car park, close to the central square of some unknown village lost in the middle of mountains that look just like all the others. This is where she lives, at Le Chamousset, a hotel with a bar and restaurant. It is a big building made of stone and wood in the local mountain style. She goes to reception to get her key. I follow, like a regular customer. We go up to the first floor. She does not say a word. That suits me. We eventually enter a room with a grey carpet and a double bed. She throws her things down on a table and I stand there awkwardly, not sure what to do. She sits on the edge of the bed and pulls off her boots. Then she opens the cupboard and produces some whisky, taking several good swigs straight from the bottle before passing it to me.

She looks at me. Her eyes seem even colder and harder than before. I take a swig before speaking.

'Does every man who chats you up get invited to your room?'

'Men usually avoid me.'

'I might want to kill you.'

'If you'd had your eyes open on the bike, you'd know that I'm not afraid of death. But if you're thinking you've come up here for anything more than a shower and some clean sheets, you're wrong. Have a drink, get washed, talk and sleep if you want to. But don't go hoping you can touch me.'

I look at her as I undress, hoping she has seen it all before. I take the hook from my belt and lay it gently on the pile of clothes. It has become my hook now. The handle is crusted with brown, dried blood. She pretends not to see the thing, even though it is huge and magnificently curved. I walk across the room to the bathroom, naked. She stares at me insistently, not deigning to look away. I find it difficult to bear. She is looking at me the way men usually look at women, complacently, delighting in it. I put the clothes in the basin to soak, and have a shower. My skin looks immaculate even though I know I am covered with the debris of everyone who has died near me in the last few days. As I stand under the scalding water, I see her come in to watch me wash.

'Don't you ever take your glasses off?' she manages at last.

She is sitting on a wicker washing basket, the whisky bottle clamped between her knees. She lights a cigarette. Soon the smoke and the steam blend into a thick fog that seems to separate us.

'Anyone who looks me in the eye pays dearly for it,' I eventually reply. 'Why have you come to watch me like this? Who are you trying to see in me? A relative? A brother? A lover?'

She is silent again for a long while, smoking and drinking, and taking her time before answering.

'It was a man, my man. My lover. Everything about him is still imprinted on me. Like something branded into my flesh. He had the same voice as you, he moved like you, had the same body, said the same things. It wasn't you, but he's come back to me through you. That's why I keep looking at you and I'm letting you stay. To know if I should carry on or start all over again.'

I stand there with the soap in my hand, puzzled. She has had too much to drink. Girls and alcohol, not a good combination. As if to confirm what I am thinking, she leans against the basin, slips and almost topples off her makeshift chair. I turn off the shower and remove my glasses so that I can look her in the eye. She looks at me and takes up my challenge. Nothing happens. She stands, comes over and puts a finger on my mouth. Her eyes are locked on to mine. I try with all my strength to delve through her to find her soul, to root it out and take hold of it. I cannot. Still she does not look away or show any sign of fear.

'I know you're not him,' she says, stroking my lips. 'You're not that much like him, actually. But when I look at you, just for a moment I feel like he's back, like he's here with me again. When he died I swore no other man would ever touch me. That was nearly twelve years ago. I haven't broken my promise and I'm not going to. I don't know why I'm helping you. Probably to make up for what happened.'

'What did happen to him?'

'I killed him. Motorbike crash. I was driving. I came away completely unharmed and he died. It was all my fault. I killed him.'

She goes out of the bathroom, taking the bottle. I dry myself, wrap the towel round my waist and join her in the bedroom. She is slumped on the sofa under a lamp, watching cartoons on television. I sit on the armrest next to her and take one of her cigarettes. She starts speaking before I have even asked her anything.

'It was in March. Winter wasn't really over, but it had stopped being seriously cold. I remember it so clearly: I'd taken out my summer gloves the moment it got milder. We were out on the bike the whole afternoon. He didn't have his licence, so I took him with me. In those days I had a yellow Daytona, a beautiful bike, all curves and almond-shaped headlights, with real British elegance. A Triumph, basically. With him behind, holding me in his arms all day long, he loved being driven by a woman: it made him feel alive. It was a really happy time in my life. Looking back it seems so puerile and pointless. That afternoon we biked to Grenoble to meet a grease-monkey friend of ours, then the three of us went to pick up a girl after she'd finished work. I've forgotten her name. She was a secretary. She hated her work. She had a Ducati 888, a perfect machine, the sort of thing only the Italians can get right. It would be a fantastic collector's piece now: red, classy, hot-tempered. I don't remember her very well, but she was full of life and laughed a lot – a bit too much for my liking, especially as she took quite a shine to my man and I'm pretty sure he wouldn't have hesitated if he'd had a chance to make a quick snack of her, on the quiet. Anyway, we had a bit of a race. I couldn't keep up. They were both very good and didn't have to think twice about anything. At the time I was pretty inexperienced and my bike was heavy. There were two of us on it, too, and so I had real trouble just keeping up. They had that knack for doing crazy things which only came to me much later. I'd already made a mess of a U-turn that afternoon and nearly come off. It must have been a premonition. On the way back to Grenoble they were going really fast and I was a long way behind. We stopped at a tiny village along the way to have a drink in a bistro and think about life, the universe and everything. At the time I hadn't yet grasped that we weren't immortal. We drank and watched the sun go down. I can remember the count exactly: two beers, one whisky and four Kirs. Twilight in March was beautiful in those days, and lasted so long.

'We finished our drinks and went our separate ways. The girl, who I've never seen again, went home with the other guy, the grease-monkey. Later they got married and had a baby. She died of a brain tumour before it was a year old. The two of us left, lovers huddled together on the bike, and I remember it stalled as I set off. That was a second warning. I was completely drunk and I knew it, but I thought that if I was careful nothing could happen. We were heading home to a big bowl of pasta and to fuck all night.

'So we set off. We rode through an industrial estate and past a railway bridge. We weren't going fast. The roads were empty and I knew every twist and turn by heart. There was a long straight stretch, then it bore round to the left. I wanted to take that bend just right, really well. I don't know what got into me, I dropped down a gear and gave it a load of throttle to get round that bastard corner as tight and fast as I could, but I'd got the wrong corner. It didn't go left but right. I didn't see anything, didn't know what the hell was going on, I was going way too quickly and I was way too drunk. I skimmed on to the verge and the bike fell on its side, we must have been going at 200. I thought, "This is it. Right now. Now I'm going to see if I die or not." I slid along on my side, still gripping the handlebars. There were these great orange sparks all around us. Then I started to fly. The headlight picked out snatches of a black, violent world with the sky crawling along beneath me. I did several somersaults and I could only think about one thing: not dying.

'It must have been written somewhere that I should live. I ended up motionless on the damp soil, in the middle of a ploughed field. The visor had come off my crash helmet. I wasn't in any pain anywhere. I called him. He didn't answer. I called again, as loud as I could. Then I looked for him, still calling quietly. He never answered. In the end I found his body, broken in two by a concrete post, a marker which said TWELVE KILOMETRES. I still remember it, that body, dead and damaged. It haunts me every day, every night and every morning at dawn. I can hear him talking to me when it's quiet and I can smell him in my sheets at night. When I saw you I thought I was having a vision, he appears like that sometimes, my gorgeous lost lover, when the pain's too much to bear.'

I stub out my cigarette in the ashtray. One more biker's story, I think.

'When you look at me what do you see?' I ask, turning towards her. 'What do you see? Do you really think I'm him?'

She turns towards me and lies down on the sofa to get a better view of me.

'When I look at you I see a tall man with dark hair, slim, quite well put together in spite of the gut, but someone who hasn't been near a razor for a while. In fact –' she stops to find the right words. She seems happy. How come she sees me as I was before, and not as I really am? When I came out of the shower five minutes ago there was still no reflection in the bay window. The last image I have of myself is the hideous face I glimpsed in Friday's eyes, up in his tower block. I would like to get close enough to her to see myself in her eyes. What will be reflected there? What will happen if I bring my face up to hers? I am afraid she will misread my intentions and react violently. I think for a while and decide that I would be risking nothing worse than a slap and nothing better than a kiss. She lifts herself up on to one elbow and looks at me. Her glass slips from her hand, falls and rolls across the carpet, spilling its contents. She keeps on looking at me now and, for the first time since we met, she flicks her eyes away for a fraction of a second. I can tell she is embarrassed.

'I'd like you to stay with me for a while. A few days maybe, just to see. I've been alone a long time now. It's hard sometimes.'

'I can't stay. I've got things to do.'

I would like to leave straight away, but I stay all the same. The afternoon goes by. We watch television and talk a bit. From time to time I get up to drink a glass of water and gaze at the mountains out of the window. Towards the end of the day she falls asleep on the sofa. I put a blanket over her so that she does not catch cold, and I carry on taking big stubborn slugs from the bottle of whisky. Her name is Hélène. She sorts apples in a factory. Hélène never knew her father and fell out with her mother, who she no longer sees and who lives further up the mountain. Hélène is sleeping. I expect I could love her, just as I suspect she loves me without daring to saying so. But I know that this is just a stop along the way. The final resting place is in some far-flung spot I have not seen yet. I am also very conscious of abusing what little time I have, and any time spent with her would seem like a suicidal indulgence.

I could have been born under different skies, on a mountainous waste-tip, still-born, or as good as. I could easily not have had the privilege of regretting what I am, nor of watching these millions of tons of granite growing pink in the fading sunlight. I think of all the lives I have not had. Hélène is still sleeping. I could of course sit down beside her, take her in my arms and press my face against hers, while I wait for the end that will surely arrive soon. I know they are on my trail, hounding me down and hungry for blood. They are coming to get me. I stay there, looking at her.

It's dark when she wakes. I am very drunk now, gripping hold of the radiator under the window, watching the motionless sky. I get dressed. She suggests having something to eat in the hotel restaurant, a huge room with irregular black floor tiles and panelled walls. There are a few people scattered about the room, eating in silence. Hidden speakers broadcast soft background music to the delight of the artificial flowers. We choose a table by the bay window and look out at the gardens and the village below us. She tells me she loves her mountains, and takes hold of my hand under the table.

'I'm glad you stayed,' she adds, as we look at the menu. 'I could feel you there all the time I was asleep. I dreamt too, and I haven't dreamt for years. I'd like to leave this place with you. We could go somewhere else, live another life in another place. Italy's not far away, we could get across the border. It's not difficult and I know the way.'

'I haven't made any decisions yet.'

We eat slowly. She lets go of my hand, but I can feel her calf against mine, and I know that this is not insignificant. She is eager for this contact which would once have had an effect on me. I no longer feel able to love, but I still feel sexual desire, like a strange urge to possess. I put down my napkin and look at her. She stares back at me. We say nothing.

'I really like you,' she manages at last.

'I know.'

'I didn't think it would ever happen again.'

'I knew it the moment I put my hand on your arm on that café terrace. Can you do something for me? I'd like to look in your eyes, to see myself reflected in someone's eyes again. Come here.'

She leans over the table, I see the soft skin on her neck, smooth and white where her blouse falls open. I take off my glasses and lean towards her. We must look like two lovers about to kiss. Then in her velvety dark irises I see myself as I was before. In her eyes I definitely am the man I always was. Who is she that she can see inside me like this? Am I different now, or just different in her eyes? I look over her shoulder and see an old woman watching me in horror. Fat tears are rolling slowly down her withered cheeks. I put my glasses back on quickly.

'What did you see?' Hélène asks, breaking the awkward silence.

'I saw myself as I really am, revealed by a woman who says she loves me. I think I understand now.'

'So you're going to stay?'

'You know I won't. I'll leave tomorrow. But I might come back for you later.'

'Will you be with me tonight, at least?'

'Yes, I'll stay. We'll sleep in the same room, so we don't feel alone. I won't touch you. I would like to have known you in another life. We would still have met, but it would have been different. Thanks to you, I feel alive again too, but I have something pretty unpleasant to admit to you: look at my reflection in that window.'

I point to the window. She turns round, sees for herself and pales visibly. A heavy silence settles over us. She slowly puts her knife and fork down and keeps her head lowered, staring at what is left of her meal. In the end she looks up and I can see her eyes are full of tears.

'Do you exist?' she asks quietly.

'Yes, but my time in this world is nearly over.'

'Am I alone at this table? Can the others see you, or are you just a dream?'

'I do exist, you'll have proof of that when the bill comes. We're eating at the same table and chosing things from the same menu. The others don't see me the way you do, though. Let's say I look like someone completely different to them. That's why I have to keep my glasses on in public. It would be far too dangerous for both of us if I took them off.'

'Let's leave, anyway. What does it matter what you are? Let's leave this evening.'

'No. We'll wait till tomorrow morning. Tonight I need to think. You need life and I'm the opposite of that.'

We finish our meal calmly. The old woman sitting opposite cannot stop crying and her family have to take her away because she is causing such a disturbance. Hélène has cried a little too. She seems better now, but she has stopped looking at me. We finish our meal and I pay.

'I don't want to go back up straight away,' she says, still looking down. 'Can we go to the bar for a bit?'

'No. I've had more than enough to drink already today. You go. I'm going up to the room. I need to sleep.'

She gives me the keys, but avoids meeting my eye, and we part without a word. I get back to the room, which is at the very end of a long dark corridor. I go in, take off my glasses and lie on the sofa. The TV is still on, but the programmes have ended. I watch the snow on the screen for a while. Grey and black snow, which neither falls nor rises, but still manages to settle in a thick layer.

I am walking through a twilight world full of volcanic ash, cinders and darkness. Dried, decomposing bodies are lined up on the ground, like fly eggs laid in another age. There is no meaning, no daylight, no wind. Nothing to breathe but this fine grey dust, which gets into everything and sticks to my eyes. My clothes have already turned the same colour as the corpses. I know that soon all I will have left to do is lie down beside them and wait. Not far away I see two of these figures lying side by side. They still seem fresh despite being covered in the same thick grey crust. Driven by some remnant of free will, I kneel down beside one of them and dust off the face with the back of my hand. It is her. I knew it would be. The lover from my dreams, lying there beside the other man. I sent them to hell, and I have followed them there. I look at her for a moment, long enough for the dust to erase her features. Just as I am about to lie down next to her, she opens her eyes. Eyes that no longer reflect anything at all.

I wake with a start on the sofa. The TV is off. Hélène has gone to bed. I can see her naked back in the light of the street lamps from the car park. The clock says five o'clock. It will soon be light. I get up without a sound, walk round the white bed and watch her sleeping. I take the hook, which I temporarily stowed on top of the cupboard, and go back over to her. I use this instrument to pull the sheet to the floor. Then I look at her for a long time, right until the sun peeps up between two mountains and sets the room alight. Then I take the key to the bike, pick up the crash helmet, and leave, making sure I close the door without a sound.

The beautiful machine is waiting for me in the car park. I take that too, flipping back the stand, undoing the Neiman and pushing the heavy bird some way away. It would be madness to fire it up in the car park: Hélène would wake to the sound of her bike as surely as a mother wakes to her baby's cry. After moving it a strenuous fifty metres, I put the crash helmet on, sit astride the machine, turn the key and press the starter button. The beauty rears up. It makes the most wonderful sound: throaty and smooth at the same time, humming a strange tune to a regular beat, a complex pattern alternating between deep basses and reedy whistling. Delicious vibrations drum up my legs and into my spine. I can feel the power of the thing through the palms of my hands. I settle myself and twist the throttle slightly. The rhythm speeds up, the notes change. I disengage the clutch with two fingers. The lever moves softly and fluidly and the sensation it affords me is a distillation of the hydraulic pleasure I can see displayed in the dial on the main cylinder. I press the gear lever gently with the tips of my toes to put it into first. It engages with a sharp thwack which makes the whole bike lurch. I lift my fingers carefully off the clutch and set off on the gentlest throttle with the sun on my back.

The road snakes round the mountain on its descent, and the machine follows it down with no surprises. The people who designed these things knew their job. In spite of the beast's considerable weight, I negotiate the hairpin bends easily. As the kilometres pass by the mountains become smaller and not so steep, the road becomes wider and straighter, and my driving more precise and aggressive. I think of Hélène and hope she will understand. If I can I will let her know where I abandon her bike, but there is no guarantee that I will be able to. Anyway, I forgot to ask her surname.

IX

EVERYTHING STARTS AT GRENOBLE. The road takes me on to a slip road and the slip road channels me on to the motorway – the real, proper motorway. I decide then to use my mount as what it truly is: a machine intended for time-travel. It was created for these smooth, wide, four-lane arteries with long, steady curves and endless straight stretches. I feel quite emotional and it is with some apprehension that I gently turn the handle. The beast roars and leaps forwards, hauling on my arm. I cling to the handlebars and lie down along the fuel tank to avoid being thrown off. The cavalry is unleashed. I stay flattened against the machine and let the charge pass by, listening to the engine singing more and more loudly as it gathers revs, until it reaches an extraordinary counter-tenor pitch that I have every intention of keeping up all the way to Paris. A quick glance at the dashboard: the needle on the speedometer is stabilising somewhere around three times the legal limit. No room for thinking, no room for day-dreaming. I have to hang on, against the wind, against the noise, against the beast itself, and hold my line between the other road users who look almost stationary. I have to anticipate obstacles, plan trajectories, foresee when I need to lean into bends or stop to refuel. I seem to be reborn as a vigilant eye, ever watchful of the world unfurling before me. The countryside springs from one distant point, drawing me in so that I cannot take my eyes off it. The whole world spills from that one spot, and I hurtle across it before it has time to take on any precise shape. All matter flows towards me, reduced to simple curves and vague outlines, geometric figures in indeterminate colours, transforming slowly before disappearing behind me.

However, on two occasions reality is reconstructed along the way. It chooses to take the form of the service stations, where I fill up with fuel in between the lorries and the saloons. Each time I set off again the structured universe disappears and reverts to a dense noisy fluid through which Paris draws ever closer. I fly through the pay toll at Fleury in the blink of an eye, and for a moment I think I can see men in blue on motorbikes. They dissolve quickly in the wing mirror and I hear no more of them. Two hours after leaving Grenoble I finally reach the Périphérique ring road, where I definitively abandon any hope of toying with the laws of the universe: the traffic has solidified here and all the vehicles seem to have clumped into one mass. So I ride carefully between two lanes along with couriers on scooters and pizza delivery boys in their brocaded uniforms.

Tired now, I decide to try my luck on the outer ring-road: bad idea. The traffic is just as slow here, but far more stressful: traffic lights, braking, changing lanes, mobile phones, dustbin lorries, crossroads, buses and intersections unite into a synergy of frustrations. I make slow progress through the frenetic teeming of this busy city, and eventually manage to get somewhere near the La Roquette area. More than once I have to slam on my brakes to spare some old woman or swerve to avoid an opening car door. I have a very clear image of the place I am heading for and I leave the bike some way short of my goal, abandoning it on a quiet grassy strip between two roads. I turn off the engine: she stops purring. Burning hot air wafts up from her overheated engine. Before leaving her, I stroke the machine one last time. She has certainly earned a rest.

I carry on on foot, crash helmet in hand, its visor smothered in midges. Will my fate be as insignificant as theirs, these tiny insects? I carry on walking. The road that I once saw by night is easily recognisable by day. I casually observe passers-by on the street. They all seem normal. They all seem relaxed. Yet I cannot help having doubts. I feel as if I am being watched. I am afraid one of them will try to rip off my mask and reveal my differences. How on earth did they turn them into these puppets, happy to follow orders? In the air, the water, the seats on the Métro? What did they do to me? What have I become without even realising it?

I cross the street, just opposite the garage where the superbike was kept. The entrance to the building is a little further on. As the days go by, I feel as if I am moving deeper and deeper into a dream, drowning in it while the real world dwindles and disappears. What sort of reality do I have a right to? A few more strides and I am beside the main door, which stands wide open in the dazzling sunlight. The caretaker, a creepy character in grey overalls, is taking the rubbish bins inside. I cross the courtyard and go up the stairs which, rather oddly, do not seem to creak by day. I go all the way to the top landing and knock on the door. Silence. I can hear muffled sounds of busy lives and echoing radios from all over the building. The whole morning streams with glorious light and bed linen hangs out of windows to air. The late summer is deploying the best of its weather, and I regret not being able to make the most of it, sitting on a terrace somewhere watching the living getting on with their carefree lives. No one comes to the door. I knock again.

'It's me,' I whisper, hearing a floorboard creak. 'I've come back to do the favour you asked for.'

The sliver of light at the spy-hole darkens for a moment. Someone is looking at me. The door opens just a crack. Baron Saturday glances at me fiercely before pulling the door wide to let me in. He is in his underpants. He holds a small revolver.

'Come in. Welcome back. I'd just gone to bed. I've been working all night. The agents are prowling around us the whole time at the moment. I'm surprised to see you again. Spirits are usually so evasive and wary, they rarely come back to the same place. I'll make some breakfast. Have you eaten?'

'No. I've come a long way.'

He puts the gun in a fruit bowl and looks at my crash helmet.

'I can see. Have you found anything out?'

'Yes.'

I sit at the table, while he puts coffee beans into an old wooden grinder. He grips the handle and starts turning.

'Do you know what maturation is?' I ask.

'You've met Dumontet, haven't you?' he says, still grinding. 'So your journey got you somewhere. When we first met I could never have told you about all that the way he has. You would never have believed me, or you would have gone mad before your time. You had to find out what you really are for yourself.'

He stops turning the handle, opens the grinder, adds some more coffee and goes back to work on it. The beans start crunching again.

'The world we used to live in doesn't exist any more,' I concede with a sigh.

'You're right. There's a new power hovering over everyone. It's cruel and it's brutal and it's everywhere, holding them all in its grip. Not one of them out there has turned their back on it. We're the last ones left to dream and the only ones who can think. I don't know why it doesn't work on us.'

'Who do you mean, us?'

'Certain African races, like the Fulani and the Diola. Their impregnation, their products, their maturation, none of it has any effect on us. We can still see clearly. I don't know why. It's just the way it is, that's all.'

Baron Saturday gets up and takes the little drawer full of coffee from the grinder, then tips it into the silver coloured percolator standing directly above the gas flame. He is an old man with skin shrivelled by the passing years, bones that stand out and vague areas of white hair scattered about his body. He walks over to the window and looks down. Then, still standing there looking out on to the street, he starts talking, almost to himself.

'At first we didn't do anything and we didn't see the storm brewing. We went from blue skies to the worst of it without even thinking of reacting. When the National Party came to power we were frightened, because we didn't know what might happen: we could lose our freedom, our dignity, we could be denied our rights. What happened next proved we were right to be afraid of them and wrong not to have fought back sooner. The arrests started, and lots of things changed: the police became much tougher and the media became much softer. Anyone who didn't submit was hunted down by those who did, and now we can see just how powerless we were at the time. We were frightened. We had to hide. We couldn't trust anyone. Then, after spending so much time shut away, we got angry. You saw what we did the other evening. You shouldn't have any regrets. It's the only way we can get them to listen to us. We're like dogs, howling for revenge by night, and curling up with a grunt during the day. All we have left is a longing to live and to kill, just so that we can exist.'

The percolator starts whistling. He pours the coffee into earthenware cups and puts a packet of biscuits on the table. We sit there in silence, gingerly sipping the scalding coffee.

'Have you got what I wanted?' I ask.

'Only some of it. We've got a stolen identity card with details that match you quite well, and we've got some information about Agnès Bouteille. She was an extreme left-wing dissident, the daughter of the Mayor of Marseilles –'

'Assistant to the Chief of Police.'

'Whatever. She was a member of the LCR and —'

'Forget it, I know all that. Do you know who made me kill her?'

'Did you kill her? You didn't tell me that. Now I understand why the Spirit world didn't want you. You've been sent back to haunt the living because you don't remember the murder, do you? Do you really think that knowing what happened that evening will bring you redemption? It doesn't say anywhere that you'll find peace like that, you do realise that, don't you?'

'I want to know, I want to understand.'

'You'll know, but don't count on understanding.'

'Who made me kill the girl?' I ask again.

'Someone called Jean Ménard. He's the man I wanted to talk to you about. You owe me a favour, if you remember.'

'Of course. I came back to honour my debt,' I say quietly before carrying on with my questions. 'How come you know so much?'

'We have a well-established network with contacts in strategic places where it's easy to get information. The Whites have regarded us as cockroaches for so long that they don't even notice us any more. All they can think about is working and earning more and more money. We're just there in the night to empty their dustbins, clean out their sewers and clean their windows.'

'Are you all black?'

'Yes, we're mostly Fulani. We see and hear a lot. We know almost everything about them, but we're like a handful of rabbits against an army of wolves. You can't afford to underestimate them. They're very powerful. Impregnation is almost complete now. I've managed to get details of the cell that the Bouteille girl belonged to. You won't be surprised to hear the LCR doesn't exist any more. All the members underwent maturation. Now they're devoted to the National Party, working meekly in its own offices. No form of resistance stood up to their poisons. When we understood what Spirits were, I secretly hoped I'd find some allies among them, but it proved impossible. You're so evasive, so transient, and you don't have time for our problems in this world. You wander about not even knowing what you're looking for. You weep and wail, following lines of force that we don't understand and waiting to be called to obscure locations. I'm really amazed you've come back.'

'How did you work out that impregnation didn't have any effect on you?'

'When our children were the only ones left in school we realised something wasn't quite right. That was when our families were sent back to Africa. That solved the problem for them.'

The telephone rings twice, two strident rings, then a weighty silence. Baron Saturday suddenly seems worried.

'We need to get back to what matters,' he says.

'All right. What is it you want me to do?'

'Remember when I told you that we are like your kind, the In-Betweens?'

I have no recollection of him mentioning this at all, so I wait to hear what he has to say. He pauses a moment, for some sign of acquiescence which is not forthcoming.

'I want everything to be clear to you,' he carries on. 'People like you usually have two options: sanctification through martyrdom or damnation through exercising your free will.'

I still say nothing, but I can already feel the threat of a monumental darkness looming over me. He waits again and looks up to the heavens before continuing.

'With you the die is already cast. There's no way you can redeem yourself. It's going to be hell whatever you do. And it won't be long before hell seems like a more attractive option than staying here.'

'Why?'

'Soon you'll be overwhelmed by your own anger. Anger and a thirst for revenge. Hell will consume you even here, in this world. Then you won't be able to get away from the agents any longer. You have to leave. You need to go back to what's waiting for you, but you should know that everything's going to happen very quickly now.'

'How do you know?'

'The way you look: you've changed a lot since the other day.'

'I'd like to know what I look like.'

'That's completely impossible,' he says. 'I wouldn't survive it.'

'What do I have to do?'

'Earn your damnation, embrace it. It's the only way.'

'The only way you know?'

'No, just the only way.'

'What do I have to do?'

'I want you to kill Ménard's family.'

He puts his empty cup on the table. It takes me a while to grasp what he has told me. To kill a family, that means killing a wife and children: the old boy is out of his mind. I try to catch his eye, but Baron Saturday has the knack, he knows how to avoid being caught. Why is he asking me to do something so appalling? Can this really be the job he was saving for me? I had not anticipated anything like this when I committed myself so lightly. I feel strangely cold and calm, even though I am horrified by the idea of perpetrating such a murder: killing a woman and children. It can't be all that complicated really. I try to get more details.

'Kill Ménard's family?'

'Yes. His wife and two daughters.'

'Children?'

'Little girls.'

'Wouldn't it be better for your cause to kill Ménard himself?'

'This isn't intended to serve our cause. We could kill Ménard if we wanted to. This is an act of pure cruelty. It's revenge, a release. We want them to understand how determined we are. They're not human any more, because they don't have a single thought of their own. They're not yet animals, because they still know what they're doing. So we want them to suffer, and it will be your deliverance.'

'That's not the way to further your cause. It won't make you look very good.'

'It doesn't matter what our cause looks like. No one talks about us. As far as the population is concerned, we don't exist. Only the National Party and the Political Police realise we're here and even then they don't know anything about us.'

'Unless your nephew speaks.'

'He didn't speak. He was dead before he got to the headquarters.'

'I can't kill children like that,' I say. 'They're innocent. This is nothing to do with them. You're asking me to commit an immoral act. You're damning yourself.'

'How can you, a Christian, talk about innocence? You who burden your own kind with Original Sin? There's no such thing as innocence. We have base desires and evil thoughts from the minute we leave the cradle. Killing these children is part of the order of things now. They're lost, anyway. They're unnatural creations brought up right at the heart of impregnation. They're living testimony of universal corruption.'

'But if you do things like that, then you're no better than the people you're fighting,' I tell him. 'You want to kill these children because the authorities killed your people, is that it? You're just like them, except you don't even have to use their chemicals.'

'We eat lambs and calves that have to be killed. Just tell yourself it's the same. Tell yourself I'm asking you to do this for some big celebration, a celebration of pain. The paschal lamb will have blond curls, that's all. I'm not asking you to chop them up into little bits. Just kill them.'

'How?'

'It doesn't matter.'

'I need to think. What will happen afterwards?'

'You won't survive it. You'll leave. I hope the Other World will have you this time.'

I look inside the coffee pot. It is empty. So I try a biscuit instead. It is a salted biscuit and, after the coffee, it tastes strange. To kill Ménard's wife and children, or rather a woman and some children, it seemed heinous at first, but now that I contemplate it again – why not? Ménard conditioned me to butcher that poor girl, and he killed my family, in his own way. He killed me, too. What Baron Saturday is suggesting is actually merely revenge, a balancing of pain. I tell myself it won't be difficult. I'll simply have to look at the children to kill them off, like the dogs on the railway tracks. For the woman and her man, we'll have to see. Is that all I came back for, back from between two worlds, from the famous Crossing of the Ways? Is it inevitable? It may well be. How can Baron Saturday justify such actions for his cause? I sit there thinking for a while, and then tell myself that he's not the first to commit massacres for the pleasure of it. It's part of human nature. I take another biscuit. They're very good.

'So, have you thought about it?' asks Baron Saturday.

'Are you sure I won't survive?'

'Positive.'

'Give me some time. I need a few hours.'

'Think it over, I'm going back to bed. But I need to make a phone call first.'

Fangiolini's phone call on the beach has left me with a bitter aftertaste. He gets up and, casually, I do the same. He heads over towards an old black telephone with a rotating dial, picks up the handset and dials a number. The contraption clicks, so does the revolver. I have picked it out of the fruit bowl and have cocked it just in case. Even though I have my back to him I am watching him in the mirror on the front of his bedroom wardrobe. He won't do what Fangiolini did, especially as he won't make the mistake of staring me in the eye. He says a few words and hangs up.

'Don't you trust me?' he asks, coming back over to me and raising one white eyebrow at the gun.

'There are some luxuries I can no longer afford. I'll lie on the sofa while you sleep.'

'I'll give you the file on Ménard, then it'll be easier for you to make up your mind. It's not difficult to get to his house. We know a lot about him.'

He goes out on to the landing and over to a fuse box, which he opens with a special handle. I follow him cautiously, gun in hand, and glance quickly over the banister into the stairwell. The long spiralling staircase looks deserted. It reminds me vaguely of an empty seashell with geometric stripes. There is a shoe box under the cables and fuses. He leafs through a wad of papers, takes out a pink folder and hands it to me. I open it while he carefully closes the cupboard. We go back into the apartment. The folder contains photographs, hand-written pages and annotated maps. It is not very thick, so I roll it up and slip it into my belt, taking out the hook at the same time. Baron Saturday looks startled. With a weapon in each hand, I lie down and cross my arms over my chest. He stands there in his underpants, looking at me as I stare at the ceiling. I am not sleepy or tired. He is irritating, standing there.

'Go and get some sleep,' I say to get rid of him. 'When you come back I will have made up my mind.'

I stay there alone, lying on the sofa. The ceiling is edged with plaster mouldings and intricate cornicing. A large copper lamp hangs from the middle of the white expanse. There is a slight draught in the room, and the heavy ceiling light sways slowly. Occasionally, as a car passes in the street, a brief flash of light illuminates the lamp, breaking into fragments of yellow all over the room. Less than a week ago I believed blindly in the world around me. I was convinced of the permanence of things and was settling down to a life without complications, free of interrogations and doubts. It was not to be. It is a week now since everything capsized. I have already lost count of how many people I must have killed.

The sound of children playing reaches me from somewhere close by, in some school playground. Probably the first break of the autumn term. What have they done to our children? Have they really banned them from dreaming so they can forge them in their own image? I get up and decide to walk outside for a while. I am going to watch the children play, to see whether what is left of me is capable of what they want me to do. The keys to the apartment are still hanging on the devil's horn. I take them and lock the door without a sound. The long spiral staircase still does not creak. In silence, I make my way down to the courtyard, which seems deep and dark now that the sun is no longer reaching into it. I go out on to the street and start walking. It is just getting warm. I check that my glasses are properly in place and follow the sound of the children shouting and laughing.

When I reach the corner of the boulevard, I stop to look. Not far away there is a bistro bathed in sunlight. I sit on the terrace. It is warm, I feel good. I order an espresso and a croissant, and an officiously stiff waiter rushes to serve me. I pay straight away and savour these few moments. People walk past: dark-haired, blond, all perfectly white, perfectly clean and very busy. They each seem absorbed in some task that will not wait. There are no drop-outs, no tramps, no beggars. Everything is as it should be, like that butcher's shop on the other side of the street. I look at the pieces of meat in pale pinks and blood reds, the rows of joints, the piles of offal, the tubs of tripe. The customers file through politely, their every move contained, their every word measured, and the people driving past are curiously polite.

I finish my coffee and leave. It will not be long before break time finishes, and I would like to see the children playing. The long high railings around the school come into view at last. The playground is deserted. I stay there a long time looking at the sand pit, the swings, the tall windows. On the roof of the school there are powerful loudspeakers broadcasting the shouts and laughter over the whole neighbourhood. I listen carefully to the soundtrack, which is playing in a loop, and try to look inside the building. Impossible to see anything, it is too dark. I grasp the railing and climb on to the little wall to get a better view. There is no one: no children, no teachers. Dazed, I climb back down and call to a passer-by.

'Look, have you seen? There aren't any children... In the play-ground here, look, it's just a recording...'

'What do you want from me? Leave me alone.'

The man walks on. A yuppie in a tie. I turn away from him and see an old woman coming towards me, pulling a shopping trolley.

'Excuse me, have you seen? The children are just a recording. Where are the children?'

She doesn't reply, walks past with her head lowered, waving her hand. I'm not trying to do bloody market research! I turn in every direction, looking for help. There's a young woman on the pavement opposite. As I cross over the bell rings for the end of break. I call the woman.

'Excuse me, did you hear that? The children's voices were a recording. The sounds from the playground and everything, the laughter, the bell, it's all on loudspeakers. Please look, for God's sake!'

She smiles at me, gives me a little nod, but doesn't seem to understand. Her eyes are vacant, her arms limp by her sides, her attitude a sham. I point at the school, and look over at it with her. The old woman and the yuppie have come to a stop on the other pavement. They're both making calls on their mobiles, looking at their reflections in an old advertising hoarding. My hand drops down. No one needs to draw me a picture. I turn back to the woman I have just spoken to: she is rummaging through her handbag.

I have nothing to gain by staying. I turn and run, head down, without a backward glance. I keep running, take a turning to the right, then the left, then right again, and hide in a cobbled side street. I can hear the long wail of mingled sirens rising over the city. Their modulated sound comes in waves, reverberating, echoing, drawing closer. A car striped with flashes of blue light hurtles past. I huddle behind a dustbin and wait.

A long time later I come out of hiding. I try to be unobtrusive, avoiding the sunshine, walking slowly, strolling as part of the crowd. Sauntering like this I manage to get back to the street where Baron Saturday lives. Three large police vans are parked by the entrance. I stop to watch. A few minutes later, a Political Police lorry comes out through the archway. I dive between two cars. They're here. They've found us.

Terror grips me now, emptying my stomach and chilling my blood. I slump to the ground, betrayed by legs that can no longer hold me. What should I do? Where should I go? What's happened to the children? A cold prickly sensation numbs my fingers and chills my mind. I look at the chrome of a bumper, deprived of my own image, and try to pull myself together: what's the point of being afraid when I'm dead anyway? Nothing worse can happen to me now. So I get up, slowly, my clothes soaked with cold sweat, and set off with my head lowered, not looking back. I am going to pick up the motorbike and try to get to the block of flats in Epinay. Perhaps they will have come back. Perhaps they will be able to hide me. I set off towards the place where I left the motorbike, but I am quickly disillusioned.

The whole square is surrounded. Agents are hurriedly trying to disperse the curious onlookers. A handful of individuals in white overalls are busy around the machine. Circling slowly, they look, observe and note down, performing a peculiar dance around the two-wheeled vehicle, which they appear to be treating with fear and reverence. I watch them searching for the one hair or trace of saliva that will match up with its owner. There is a truck waiting to take the beautiful creature to God knows what laboratory somewhere. It seems highly unlikely Hélène will ever see it again.

Other agents are questioning the gawpers around me. How on earth do they manage not to notice me? The closest of them is within touching distance, but he does not seem to see me, or does not want to turn towards me. I sigh and retrace my steps once more, heading back to the apartment. The street is deserted. I sidle along the walls. It is very hot and I step gratefully into the comparative cool of the building. I climb the now familiar staircase once again. There is a heady smell coming from the upper floors, carried on a slight draught. I reach the top landing: the fuse box has been broken open and the shoe box has disappeared. There are seals over the doors. I pay no attention to them, take out the key and open the door. The seals snap with a little sound like a biscuit breaking. The smell is stronger here, hot and heavy. Everything looks orderly. I go in and close the door behind me. The apartment is deserted, it doesn't appear to have been searched. I get a glass of water from the kitchen and stand there for a moment, looking out of the window. I put the glass down, walk across the living room and inspect the bedroom. The bed is made and the wardrobe empty. There is a cup on the bedside table. I go to the bathroom to pee, open the door and understand the smell: I should have guessed really.

There is blood everywhere. In the bath, on the floor, on the ceiling. Everywhere. Litres and litres of blood splattered all over the room. The basin is full of extracted teeth. I close my eyes and go back out, leaving big, sticky footprints on the floor. Baron Saturday is no more. What the hell can they have done to him? I sit down on the bed for a moment to catch my breath. I'll do what he has asked of me. These men deserve revenge. I'm going to kill that woman and those children. I'm going to set myself free.

I still have the gun tucked into my trousers. I take it out and look at it. A small revolver. A black Smith & Wesson. There are four bullets in the cylinder. I have barely finished counting them when the door of the apartment opens. Two agents come in. They're wearing heavy grey bullet-proof clothing with matching helmets and boots, and holding their weapons at hip level. They're slow to react: I see the surprise in their eyes. Without a flicker of emotion I aim at one, then the other, and bring them down. Two projectiles to pierce two skulls. The blood spouts twice. The image of Dumontet's shattered head comes back to me. The effect here is very different: no great loss of tissue, no exploding of the skull or geysers of blood, just two little holes, two little jets of blood, *basta*. It's all a question of ballistics, I suppose. The two bodies are slumped untidily on the floor. As he fell, one of the agents broke the coffee table. I leave everything as it is, get up and walk out, taking my hook and the two remaining shots. When Friday comes home, he'll see that his father didn't die in vain.

I close the door without a sound and go out to wander the streets for a while. I need to find somewhere quiet and safe to have a quick look at the Ménard file. As I walk up and down I finally realise that there are no children anywhere. Still, I look for them obstinately, in playgrounds and leafy squares, in shops and in the street: in vain. No pregnant women, no tiny babies, no children, no pushchairs or prams. Just recorded squeals in a curiously silent city.

I am hungry. Before I decide what to do I need to eat. I know I do not have much time left and that is why I come to a halt in front of a smart-looking restaurant. Its dark green façade is partly masked by a thick vine laden with white grapes. The establishment offers a gourmet menu written in careful calligraphy, framed in gold and boasting astronomical prices. A series of cassolets, mixed grills and fricassees bolstered by pompous, mouth-watering descriptions. I suddenly long for that brand of hushed calm: I go in. It has an expensive atmosphere and thick carpeting. The head waiter comes to take my coat and things, but I have nothing. I counter his aloofness with my own contempt. I choose a table, then ask to change to another. It is a huge room with arches along the ceiling supported by narrow columns of white marble. On the walls there are Spanish paintings of hunting scenes. I ask to change tables again, claiming there is some sort of smell. The waiters quickly oblige, contorting into reverential bows and submissive gestures, which make them look like great white worms writhing on the ground. I move the cutlery out of my way, tuck into the canapés and take the file from my belt. The waiter behind me pretends not to notice. I am just opening the file when they bring me the menu. I choose straight away and inform the wine waiter of my choice at the same time before starting to read.

Ménard lives on the Avenue Foch, in an eighteenth-century private mansion with a garden. The page is illustrated with two photographs and a drawing. They show the façade and the garden of a magnificent town house, and a sketch of the floor plan. They also show six heavily armed guards on duty, along with a string of CCTV cameras. Fort Ménard is more impregnable than Fort Knox. Mind you, he does work for Special Operations. He is director of all experimental programmes, but the file does not give any details about his work. It is, however, very detailed, considering it has been put together by road-sweepers and dustmen. There is a short résumé of our man's life: forty-three years old, born in Paris, a doctorate in organic chemistry, married for twelve years (photo), member of the National Party for fifteen. Two daughters (photos), two cars (photos), two houses (photos). The second house catches my attention. The Ménards spend almost every weekend on a country estate in the Yonne region, about a hundred kilometres from Paris; a place reserved for the Party elite. It is Saturday today, what luck.

The asparagus roulades have arrived. I stop reading and taste them: perfection. I do not betray my gastronomic delight, and maintain the same neutral expression when the wine waiter asks me to taste his 300 bottle of wine. I wave him away and let the combination melt in my mouth, aware that these will be the last moments of physical pleasure of my entire existence.

The estate that the Ménards go to is described in detail and illustrated with several drawings and photographs. The woods have been landscaped to include a golf course, tennis courts, swimming pools, a sauna, riding stables and more besides. There is a collection of small, opulent villas dotted about to house the highest ranks of the governing bodies, bringing them together in a place where they can relax without having to associate with the populace. A large red cross indicates my client's house.

'Is anything wrong, sir?' says a waiter.

I look around. There is nothing to disturb me.

'Was the asparagus not to your liking?' he goes on.

I understand. After the first couple of mouthfuls, I became absorbed by the information and sketches, and my first course is now cold, surrounded by solidified sauce.

'Could you have my plate warmed up,' I say pointing to it, 'and don't speak to me again.'

The waiter is a professional, he does as I ask without even the quiver of an eyebrow. I go back to my reading, while he takes the plate away. There is no floor plan for this house. On the other hand, there is a very old publicity leaflet, which gives me a pretty clear idea of what the whole estate will be like. Before becoming a military base it was a huge leisure park intended for city people who needed a dose of chlorophyll, but loathed the countryside. There are touching photographs of children laughing and playing in a swimming pool, and of an elderly man brandishing a golf club against the backdrop of a green in touched-up colours.

The file gives details of a bus route, from Place d'Italie in Paris, which stops in the nearby village of Savigny. Lastly, there is a recent Polaroid of the entrance to the estate as it will appear to me. The photo is rather dark and out of focus, probably taken in a hurry, but it shows a huge gate raised like a guillotine and surrounded by hedges of barbed wire, massive watchtowers, poised to drench nocturnal intruders with light, and soldiers with Kevlar breastplates pacing up and down along electrified fences.

My dish comes back, warmed by some minion in the kitchen. I close the file and eat properly this time. I drink too, intoxicating myself with good food and wine, with brandy and cigars, until the painful bit comes at last. I still have the taste of fricassee of *petits-gris* snails with figs in my mouth as I count out the money. I leave no tip, but get to my feet and stagger slightly. The corpses of two bottles of wine eye me from the table. A third is in its death throes in the ice bucket. I finish it off, drinking straight from its mouth, and leave. The waiters form a guard of honour for me, overwhelming me with thanks before closing the door. I am out on the pavement, alone again. I have made my decision: I am going to Place d'Italie. I hate buses. I think I will take the Métro instead.

I end up taking the bus though, after a glance at the entrance to the Métro proved I can no longer tolerate underground travel. With its tortuous green metal shapes, it seemed to be luring me in like a voracious anemone. So I stand patiently on the pavement, waiting for one of those great articulated vehicles. There are other people with me at the bus stop. An old woman with a little grey bun, holding her handbag like the Queen, glances at me cautiously from time to time. But the one who truly worries me is a young man in a denim jacket with an MP3 player that I can hear hissing from where I stand. He really is watching me. He does not realise that I am watching him too, from behind my dark glasses. I suspect he has worked out what I am. In spite of the piercings, he looks and behaves like a shrewd, intelligent man. I decide I will kill him straight away if he takes out his mobile. For a brief moment the old woman and the young man look at each other, and I could swear there is some sort of complicity in their eye contact. I sit down on a metal flip-up seat. The bus is taking its time.

We are joined by a man of about forty with greasy hair, jeans, black leather jacket and white T-shirt. He nods to the young man. Why are they greeting each other like that? Is this some recognised sign? Do they know each other? Are they neighbours? Do they meet often? Or are they giving each other a sign for a different reason? The man in the leather jacket stays standing. He glances up the street at regular intervals, as if looking out for the bus, or for reinforcements of some sort. I start feeling anxious. On the other side of the road there is a man waiting at the wheel of a parked car. His window is open and he is just sitting there, waiting and watching the street.

I stand up and feel the cold hard weight of the revolver through my clothes. Four agents, two bullets, plus the hook, just in case. I'll be needing it for this job. But I'd rather kill them without using any sort of blade, especially this one. It's too medieval for this city setting. I slip my hand under my sweatshirt, grip the revolver, and get ready to take a pot-shot: one, two. I could get them easily, I just need the right technique. They're very close and it would be no problem getting a bull's eye at chest height. Still, I'd rather aim for the head, it's more guaranteed, more radical, and more profession-al in a way, though it's harder to aim accurately at a skull. I've only got two bullets. Two bullets to burst two balloons and win a teddy bear. Let's get on with it.

I am woken from my thoughts by the huge reptilian bus, which comes to a halt in front of us, blocking out the sun. The people waiting suddenly seem to lose interest in me and get on without a backward glance. I follow them. I must be losing my mind. I was about to kill those poor people. I buy a ticket and head for the back, determined to keep my calm now. My crew of three are sitting together, catching each other's eyes, but not talking. The bus is huge, comfortable, silent. This is an off-peak period. I am the only person standing. No one is reading, no one is looking out of the window. They all just sit there, motionless, staring into space with their hands on their knees. There is something abnormal about this new city I am gradually discovering. A city without chil-dren. A city without conversation. A city which has become a multitude of prying eyes touching me and frisking me – yes, because they all seem to be watching, their cold expressions crawl-ing over me like so many chilled slugs.

No chance of carnage here: even half empty, the bus easily carries three dozen people. I would do better to stay close to an exit and keep an eye on what they do and when they get up. A mobile rings. It startles me. Two people stare at me. A man takes out his handset and answers it. He only says a few words before hanging up. If he turns round, I'll blow his head off. He turns round. I get a grip of myself and decide to wait until the last moment. Nothing happens.

The city flits by, we go up, down, and cut across wide, busy main roads and little squares with cool fountains. Then the Seine at last, slow and brown, trundling the mountains down to the sea day after day. The bus sways lazily as it goes up the Boulevard de l'Hôpital, running parallel to the grey girders of the overground Métro. Place d'Italie, finally. I feel calm. I get out and go over to the ticket office to pay my bus fare. I buy a one-way ticket to Savigny and walk across to some caryatids carved into pillars to drink from a trickle of water.

It is hot. I get into the waiting bus and the air inside is stifling. I sit at the back, against the window, and watch the seats fill up, one by one. Lots of people are in smart clothes. I assume they are going home, back to the country. A big fat man with a blotchy face sits quite close to me. Stocky, hefty, his neck is thicker than a bull's. He has big hands, calloused from working the fields. Time has whitened his thick moustache, bleached his blue eyes and stooped his back. He is wearing brown corduroy trousers, which match his jacket, and a thick shirt in coarse cotton. He puts a plastic bag down carefully on his lap and takes out a small leather-bound book with a scarlet page-marker hanging from it. His thick yellowed nails stand out against the white paper. What did he come up to the big city for? I ruin my eyes trying to make out the title on the page: 'John 13:18'. Why not? I am amazed it is permitted, and I speculate about the subversive nature of the material.

The bus has filled up, and the driver gets in. He lets the engine warm up and puts on the air conditioning, which chills me to the bone in a matter of seconds. Then two agents step into the bus, and look us up and down. My head instantly empties of all thought. I can feel the ends of my fingers shaking. The two men in long blue leather coats inspect the passengers one by one. I hadn't anticipated this. Any unauthorised travel is monitored. I stay at the back of the bus, not moving a muscle, waiting. Each person shows their ticket and their identity card, and the agents slide them through a scanner. They verify them very quickly. They're heading inexorably closer to me. What should I do? What can I show them? My false ID card? The Party card? Both? No, not both, they're not in the same name. They're very close to me now, and the nearest agent asks the man reading his Bible for his papers. The man looks up just as the agent is looking down at him. He must have been absorbed in his reading and didn't hear them. Yes, there's a little hearing aid behind his ear. He hasn't heard anything, or seen anything either. Startled, the old country boy snaps his book shut. The agent tries to take it from him.

'Give me that!'

The old boy is quicker than he looks. Fat though he may be, he lands a lightning blow on the agent, striking him on the chin and lifting him clean off the ground. He falls back down flat on his back and doesn't move. The old man is a hard nut, brought up on sturdy country pâté and eau-de-vie. His fists are like rocks, his eyes like steel, but the agents are professionals and, without batting an eyelid, I watch the one still on his feet take out his electric truncheon. The old man tries his best to force his way out, parrying the blow with his Bible, without effect. The flash of blue light burns his nervous system and blinds me for a moment. A strong smell of burnt pig sweeps through the bus. Everyone is calm. I force myself to be too. The old boy is lying in the central aisle, the smouldering book in his hand.

'That's it, ladies and gentlemen,' the agent announces, putting away his weapon. 'Thank you for your cooperation. A team will be here in a few minutes, then you'll be able to leave.'

To leave. There's only one thing I want to do: leave. But I force myself to stay sitting, like the others, to show nothing. Time passes, some men arrive at last, take a few photos and put the two bodies into big black plastic bags. Then they leave, like everyday collectors of human refuse. The bus doors close and silence falls: we set off.

X

THE BUS PICKS UP THE MAIN road heading south. It is a comfortable, modern vehicle with large red letters on the back window proclaiming its technological refinements. I gradually manage to unwind and make the most of the quiet. Luckily for him, it did not occur to the agent to carry on with his inspection. I try to turn my mind elsewhere.

As we travel along, I think of the past glory of this major highway, which became a secondary road once the motorway was built. In each little town I feel almost nostalgic at the sight of expensive hotels that were once essential staging posts but, with no customers and no one to restore them, are now reduced to drab, dirty blockhouses. One particular building attracts my attention and elicits my pity. In its prime it must have been a magnificent hotel-restaurant with white walls and a steeply pitched roof extending over the long wing of guest rooms. The place is dead and abandoned now. The lawns have gone to seed and the car park is pock-marked with potholes. The yellowing façade, punctuated with dark orifices without windows or doors, makes the former restaurant look obscurely like a dry, empty skull, disappearing from sight as the bus carries me away. We travel through anarchic towns, sliced cruelly in half by the road, and, closing my eyes for a moment, I stream towards the country, like blood flowing from a wound.

There is a storm brewing in the west and for a large part of the journey I sit motionless, gazing at massive cumulonimbus clouds rolling towards the bus, threatening shadows of the towers of Babel rearing up to meet us. At one point the rumbling clouds devour the sun and everything goes dark. The lights come on inside the bus, but everyone is looking outside. The storm is directly above us. A deluge of rain and hailstones rattles against the windows like steel balls. Squalls make the whole bus sway, and at times the driver seems to lose control.

It is not far to my stop now. The loudspeaker announces it. We are slowing down already. I rise to get off in this new place masked by heavy curtains of rain. The door opens and folds aside silently. I can just make out a vague village and some ghostly houses. I get out and walk the short distance to the bus shelter. Three teenagers are lounging on a bench, keeping an eye on their scooters and smoking, but not saying a word. I step out of the rain and huddle in the shelter beside them, waiting for the downpour to stop and knowing that they are saying something about me with their meaningful glances. I turn round and look them up and down.

They must be fifteen: ravaged with acne, a hint of down on their chins. They are having a go at doing nothing and seem to be enjoying it.

'Hell of a storm, innit?' prompts the one with the cigarette.

'Yes. I'm looking for the Savigny Estate. Do you know where it is?'

'That way.'

'Is there an ironmonger's in the village?'

'Yup. Old Mrs Snatch. Over there, beyond the little bar.'

'Is that really her name?'

'No.'

'Give us a cigarette and a light,' I tell him, and the kid does as he is told, lighting a cigarette and handing it to me. I nod my thanks and take a long drag. Then I look at them: they are uncomfortable. A flash of lightning suddenly illuminates the inside of the bus shelter, followed almost immediately by a jolting clap of thunder, which thumps me in the chest and almost finishes me off.

'Fuck me, that was close!' says the boy, jumping to his feet.

I look outside for a moment, dazed. The massive thunderclap has set off a car alarm, which yells its two-tone wail to an indifferent world. I take a step forward, look up at the sky and stub out my cigarette.

'I think I'm being followed. Better not hang around here.'

I decide to set off, despite the rain. If some master of the skies wants to take me, then let him get on with it. The church is streaming with water, pouring from every gargoyle. I cut across a deserted car park fenced in by houses with closed shutters and planted with a little crop of telephone kiosks. The shop is about a hundred metres away. I walk by the bar without slowing my pace, but just glimpse the drab light of a single neon bulb, standing in for a tropical sun for a few winos propping up the bar. The sawdust on the floor is their sand, the bar counter their beach. They are sunbathing.

I carry on past these tourists of life and eventually come to the tiny ironmonger's shop. The name *Snatchbull* is painted on a chipped sign. Old Mrs Snatch: fate dealt the poor woman a bit of a blow. An anonymous and ill-intentioned hand has scrawled a loud 'Go, Snatch, go!' on the wall. I go in and a little bell rings. The shop is small and old-looking. It smells of dust, birdseed and engine oil and is filled from floor to ceiling with shelves, display units and piles of goods – everything anyone could ever need, aside from clothes or food. The area of uncluttered floor space can be measured in footsteps: three or four along, one across. There are rows of packets, boxes and sachets along the floor and piled up, lining the walls, multitudes – it would be pointless trying to count them. Nails, screws, tools, appliances, paints, fillers, electrical accessories and flue brushes of every possible size fill Mrs Snatchbull's cave of wonders.

A bedside light on the counter gives off a feeble yellow glow: the only residual light between two blinding flashes of lightning. The thunder rattles the window panes and the rain lashes the door. I stay there alone for a while, looking at the piles of merchandise. Then at last a door opens at the very back of the shop and an ageless little woman appears. She glides towards me without a sound.

'Good afternoon,' she says, and time seems to be set in motion again. 'Can I help you?' she adds, courteous and polite with a steady, slightly nasal voice.

'Hello, yes. I'd like to buy some wire-cutters please.'

'Of course, sir. What is it you need to cut?'

'Fencing.'

She turns round, picks up a stepladder, opens it and climbs up. I am unsettled by the neutral tone of our conversation. I feel truly dead at that moment. The stepladder is for sale. The woman is wearing carpet slippers. I watch her. She is decrepit, covered in the same dust as her goods. Under her faded, flowery overall, I know that she was once young and beautiful, before she wilted over the years. Now, at the very top of the shelves, almost skimming the ceiling, she takes out a flat, grey case, which she brings down and lays on the counter. She opens it: inside is a series of increasingly large apertures cut out of the foam. Each one houses its own pair of pincers, all identical except for their size, which range from major engineering to surgical. Black steel, sharp jaws, red handles: I look at them admiringly. She shows them off with pride, tilting the case towards me with a nod, hoping for a sign of approval or whistle of admiration. But nothing comes. I look up.

'I'll take the whole case.'

She closes it carefully, her eyes sparkling. She keys the figure into a calculator, the phosphorescent green digits reflected in her eyes.

'Ninety-two euros and forty-five centimes, please sir.'

'There you are,' I say, taking out the notes.

'Thank you, sir.'

She hands me the case and I take it from her. I now look like a travelling salesman. I turn around and head for the door, but it is still raining just as hard. Before leaving, I think again and turn back: I have not quite finished yet.

'Sorry to bother you, but which way is it to the Savigny Estate?'

She hesitates for a moment, not for long, but time enough for me to notice. For days now I have had to watch every detail like this. I am beginning to see what goes on in people's hearts, even if they are old and dry.

'Turn right out of the shop,' she says, 'and carry on till you come out of the village. Then follow the signs for the motorway. The entrance to Savigny is about five kilometres away, just the other side of the woods. What are you doing at the estate?'

'Going to see some children. Goodbye.'

'Goodbye, sir.'

I open the door and the bell rings again. I go out, close the door and set off under the driving rain. The village looks grey and gloomy. The lights are on in some of the houses. I glance through their windows and the interiors look drab and outdated. I keep my sunglasses on and trip occasionally, because I can hardly see a thing. I follow the old woman's instructions as best I can, and they bring me to the outskirts of the village where I pass a sign with the word SAVIGNY crossed out with a line of red.

I take off my dark glasses and slip them into my pocket, but the world seems hardly any lighter. The deserted road cuts across a vast plain where a tractor is ploughing slowly. The heavy machine comes towards me, then turns round on the earth track that runs alongside the road. The huge steely ploughshares tear through the grassy skin to lay bear the earth's entrails. I step off the road and on to the track parallel to it, reassured by the feeling of soft mud under my feet. It is invigorating, giving me new confidence, healing my sadness and filling me with hope. The tractor has turned round and is trundling away. Soon it will be reduced to a dot on the horizon, obstinately getting on with its scarification until the whole plot is a huge wound. We must injure the earth to make it fertile, flay it before it gives birth to anything.

Overhead, the storm is gliding gradually eastwards. The lightning is becoming fainter and the thunder moving away. The afternoon feels a little lighter, but I know that the darkness has only receded the better to descend. It will soon be night and every trace of light will disappear. Walking on the sodden path proves hard work. The ground sticks to me, wants me. It wants me to be carried away and clings to my feet, so I have to drag a thick layer of cloying soil on my shoes. I keep slipping, twisting my ankles and struggling to lift the heavy clods, which I try repeatedly to scrape off with the hook, but I cannot. I resign myself to carrying this cargo of thick sticky mud, which trips me up with almost every step.

A few hundred metres ahead the road goes into the woods. Old Mrs Snatchbull was right. I carry on, one step at a time, listening to the distant groan of the tractor, as if it were a cheering crowd. When I reach the edge of the woods, the track turns right and skirts round the trees, so I get back on to the road and crouch to scrape down my soles. I remove the brown clay with meticulous care, making a little pile of it next to me. Suddenly the pile is illuminated by a yellow glow which makes me look up. Far away in the west the setting sun has finally dropped below the clouds. The woods light up with sparkling gold and the clouds to the east form a fiery blaze streaked with lightning. I stay there for a while, looking at the sky. Back where I have come from all the lights are out in the village. My shoes are clean. I get up and go into the woods, just as the sun dips down for the night. So be it.

I keep walking. It has stopped raining, but the sounds of rain are still all around me in the woods. The road is deserted, the case rather heavy. An elegant vault of branches towers above me and I feel as if I am advancing through an endless green tunnel. I wade through the leaves in the undergrowth – they do not stick to me or make a sound. I cover about a kilometre like this, perhaps two, and I allow myself a pause to drink from a little stone fountain, probably the vestige of some pilgrim trail. Three newts are writhing at the bottom of the water. I watch them for a moment, and then set off again, but not for long: a few dozen metres on, a whole expanse of the forest has been cut to the ground. Only a handful of large trees are left, sturdy and upright amid piles of logs marked with fluorescent spray paint. But what interests me is not this area of bare land, but what lies beyond it. The far edge of this open expanse is marked by a double barbed-wire fence, which separates the felled trees from an immaculate stretch of grass. Another golf course. Coming back to where this all began, I feel as if I have gone round in circles and everything I have done has been pointless. I stop and think. It is the Savigny Estate golf course. I remember seeing it on Baron Saturday's map.

I leave the road and cut across the naked expanse in the encroaching darkness. I fall twice, tripping over tree stumps that seem to have been left there deliberately to catch me out. I get up, twice, then stop in front of the first fence, which must be a good five metres high. It is made from fine wire mesh and solid posts, with great rolls of barbed wire along the top. Between the two fences there is a sandy no man's land about ten metres wide. I can see the tracks left by patrolling vehicles perfectly clearly, but of course I don't see the umpteenth tree stump put in my path by some evil spirit. I flounder and fall heavily to the ground, noisily snapping twigs beneath me.

I lie there on the leaves for a moment, exhausted. Just as I am about to get up I hear the dog panting: they're coming. I stay on the ground, flattened and motionless in the growing darkness. Three men appear to my left. They are patrolling between the two fences with a dog, carefully checking with a torch to see that the fencing is intact. The dog stops, raises its nose and sniffs. The men pause with him and watch. Everything stops. I feel I am tasting eternity. At last they set off again. The dog didn't smell me any more than the guards saw me.

I sit on the ground waiting for a long while, until it's completely dark. The stars have driven away the storm. I get up, covered in leaves and moss, like the scarecrow from *The Wizard of Oz*, the Down's syndrome version. I remove the worst of the vegetation stuck to me. The sunglasses have broken in my pocket and I try in vain to reassemble the various parts. In the end I abandon the fragments. I won't need them any more, anyway. I pick up the case and go over to the fence, not knowing how long it will be before the patrol comes back or other guards pass. I put the case on the ground and open it. I am still not sure why I decided to buy all of the wire-cutters. I choose a middle-sized pair, they feel cold and heavy. I grasp them firmly and cut my first piece of fence.

Everything is black, as uniform as black velvet spread before my eyes, and yet, as I stare blankly at this abyss, I see the stars piercing it gradually – at first the brightest, then a multitude of dots so pale they seem to form vague luminescent clouds. Gradually the outline of the trees emerges against this celestial background. My eyesight is coming back. I am lying on my back, my hands are burnt, my arms hurt. I don't know what voltage they put through that fence, but I should have been more cautious: you can't get to the Powers that Be that easily. The pincers are still hanging from the fence, soldered to the wire. It was naïve of me to think I could just cut out an opening and step inside. I sit down, dazed. I still want to get in, but I need to rethink my method. I could try to bring a tree down on to the fence, but I don't have the right tools. I could pole vault over, but that seems a bit ridiculous. In the end I decide to try my luck again. I take another pair of wire-cutters and wrap the handles in the foam lining from the case, which, unlike my clothes, is perfectly dry. I touch the fence with the tip of the cutters: it's fine.

I start cutting away an opening about one metre square. I take my time about it. I concentrate, working carefully and steadily. I have to bend my body into an unnatural position, so I am soon stiff and uncomfortable. Pausing for a moment, I look around and notice the little porcelain contacts isolating the fencing itself from the posts. I could have avoided a nasty experience if I had made this detailed inspection before offering myself as its earth. The job needs me: I go back. The wires give way, one by one, with a dull snap. I carry on, relentlessly sketching out an opening. I really hope it doesn't start raining again before I finish. After many minutes of laborious effort I finally take out the area of fencing, put away the cutters, close up the case and step carefully through the gap. I'm in. I still have the second fence to get through, but I've got the knack now, it will be quick.

As I am kneeling in front of the second fence with the cutters in my hand a brief flash of lightning makes me look round. They're over there, 200, 300 hundred metres away. I can see their torches. They're coming back. I stiffen, think I should run, hesitate. Will I have time to cut out a big enough opening before they get to me? I set to work, frenetically this time. The cutters slip from my hand and fall. I pick them up and carry on cutting. They fall again. A cat flap, I just need a cat flap to slip under this fence. Every link of the thing is set against me, every piece of wire resists my efforts. A painful, invisible death flows through it. I have to finish this quickly, so I take risks, working too hastily, and soon enough, the speed punishes me. The thing that was bound to happen suddenly happens: I lose my grip, the foam slips off the handle, and my hands come into direct contact with those cold conducting cutters. Cutters that are now tightly closed on a thick wire throbbing with electricity. My time is up.

I open my eyes again, my hands still clamped on the tool. Nothing happened. The fence has no current. Implacable logic, I realise. It would be incredibly stupid to put a lethal fence within reach of important people. The dog has started barking. He isn't far away now. I cut a few more wires, pull off the section of fencing and hurl it away, then flatten myself and wriggle through, my head almost touching the ground, writhing like a fat caterpillar. They're really close now. I'm getting through, with my arms pinned to my sides. Their voices are coming nearer. In a few seconds they'll see me and shoot. Guaranteed. I come out on the other side of the fence at last and stand up as if shedding a skin. Then I run like a madman towards the woods.

That is when I hear them shout. I can hear strange whistling sounds that chill my blood and deaden my legs, but still I keep running, then dive into the dark vegetation. Time is running out. They'll raise the alarm. There's no shelter for me now, no refuge. I feel my way through the trees, tripping and steadying myself on trunks slick with humidity. For a moment a fleeting glimmer of light from the distant sky affords me a shimmering glimpse of the spongy undergrowth, pitted with potholes and waterlogged ruts. The storm is coming back. Some bloody evening.

Far behind me the shouting and whistling have stopped. They must be waiting for me somewhere else. I carry on for a while, taking pot luck with the ruts and tree trunks, making the most of the brief flashes of light coming from the advancing clouds. In the end I lose all sense of left and right, up and down. I bump into things, trip, fall and fall again until I have no sense of direction at all. I pause for a while. I put my arms around the trunk of a large chestnut tree, which gives me an idea of verticality, and wait there for a moment, listening to the sky rumbling overhead. When I feel ready to walk again I let go of the huge tree and set off, haphazardly pursuing the route I was taking until, finally, I glimpse lights through the branches. I start running towards them. They're not far away, small street lamps lining a road through the woods edged with a low, gravelled pavement. The lamps have big blue luminous globes, which shed a generous amount of light and turn the leaves on the trees an improbable navy blue.

I stay under cover, but move closer to the lights to consult the map. It's wet and difficult to read. The roads on the estate are oddly laid out, apparently forming a series of loops around a core, like several layers of petals. The principal leisure activities are concentrated in the middle of the flower, except for the golf course, which is well outside this harmonious corolla. I must be on the road that leads out to it – the flower's stem, you could say. I look at the sky. The storm is definitely coming from the west, so north must be to my left. I come out of the woods and walk along the pavement towards the centre of the flower: I'm going to gather the nectar from those little girls' heads.

The fine gravel crunches underfoot as I follow the aimless curves of the road. Huge puddles reflect the street lamps. I eventually come to the first houses, strange low-slung buildings with wooden verandas. They are all built to the same design, bungalows with big bay windows, their well-tended lawns surrounded by thick, dark hedges. A very large proportion of the houses look locked up, some are abandoned or in ruins. I arrive at the first crossroads. All the roads are identical. No signs, no names, the same harsh bluish light everywhere. The estate seems deserted, abandoned by all human life. No cars, no lights from windows, no one in the street, no movement.

Just as I think time is standing still, the wind rustles through the branches and the first raindrops start to fall. I take out the map. I am lost. The map is reasonably helpful, but the water falling on it erases it completely and it is just a ball of papier mâché by the time I discard it in the gutter. It's not important. I need to go left and then right. I cross the road and carry on. The rain is falling heavily now, making the woods whisper all around. I listen to their hoarse muttering about buds and leaves and gullies, their stories punctuated with the roar and rumble of the skies. I let the singing waters lull me. Tiredness is catching up with me and it is not long before a sweet torpor spreads through me. I am asleep on my feet.

I come back to reality with a start: a dark car has just drawn up beside me. It carries on at walking pace, overtakes me and stops. Two men get out. I didn't see or hear anything. The car has a revolving light on the roof. A bad sign.

'Good evening, sir,' says one of the men as they come over towards me. 'Can we help you?'

'Good evening, gentlemen, Jules Ménard.'

They glance at each other.

'Look at the state I'm in,' I go on. 'I was at the fourteenth hole when a Black attacked me, beat me up and took everything – even my car, so I'm getting home under my own steam. I'm glad you're here: you can take me to my brother's house.'

They stand squarely in front of me and train a torch on my face. I watch them fall apart.

'Oh fuck! It's one of them!' the one on the right screams.

I drag their bodies into the woods. They died a stupid death, victims of their routine jobs, I suppose. Without my glasses it's difficult to lie about what I really am – and impossible for them to survive the hold I have on their souls. They are sturdy boys, fit, well-trained, and strapped into dark all-in-one uniforms. It is a struggle getting rid of them, so I leave them to the kind attentions of the woodland animals. I get into their car. It's hot inside. The radio crackles. I find one of their long blue leather coats on the parcel shelf, take all my clothes off and put it on. I also take off my old trainers, which are waterlogged. Then I get into the driver's seat and set off.

I congratulate myself for this interlude out of the rain, because the house is a good deal further than I thought. It is just like all the others, except it has two agents guarding the door, gleaming like stone statues in the rain and quite difficult to spot. I do not slow down, but wave to them as I pass. They nod in reply. I thought so: the rain is so heavy they cannot see a thing. I carry on driving slowly down the street, hoping I can get rid of the car as soon as possible. A clear, loud voice suddenly booms inside the car: the radio has stopped hissing.

'Car 12, this is control. Could you debrief on your intervention, over?'

Startled, I have to think quickly. Am I car 12? I glance at the dashboard, which gives away nothing useful on the subject. There are a few pieces of paper hanging from a clip. It is too dark and the writing's too small for me to make out. The two agents must have radioed to say they had seen a stranger before getting out and stopping me. This must be car 12. I pick up the handset and press the little red button on the side.

'Control, this is car 12. Nothing to report, over.'

I turn and stare stupidly at the radio. They're now asking me to identify myself. What should I do? What should I say? I feel helpless. I prevaricate and ram the car into a bollard. The engine stalls.

My strategy didn't last long. Now I'm trapped. I turn the key and start the car again, decide not to answer and carry on going with all my lights out. The storm is overhead. With every flash of lightning the radio gives a squall of static. Thunder roars and crashes around me like the waves of a furious sea. What do I care? The car agrees to reverse up on to the lawn and skates all the way to an impressive forsythia, before getting bogged down in the mud. I turn off the engine just as fat hailstones start rattling on the windscreen. I wait for a while until this machine-gun fire from the sky is replaced by fine rain. Then I open the door and get out.

The car has come to a stop in the middle of an ornamental pond covered with undulating lily pads. I walk across it, the water up to my knees, wading laboriously towards the bank, then head back towards the road. I pad barefoot through the wet grass, which exhales an acid smell with every footstep, a smell that hangs in the air. I crouch down between the stones lining the drive and watch the road. The raindrops are falling in heavy drifts, creating layers like muslin veils in front of the street lamps. Now and then a violent flash of lightning illuminates every last detail with almost obscene intensity, revealing even the underskirts of the most insignificant shrub.

There is no one around. I run across the road and dive into the garden opposite, melting back into the shadows. I carry on like this, flitting from one garden to the next, towards the Ménards' house with its sentinels of stone. There are no fences between the plots, but there are tall thuya hedges, like walls of green concrete that I can easily get through. I must be very close now. I choose a dark corner to huddle in and look out at the manicured lawn, the white statues and the precious rose bushes. The garden is well tended. The lights are on in the house. Occasional flashes of lightning from the sky betray the two men standing stock still by the door, keeping watch. They are the ones who waved to me a few minutes ago. Perhaps they were tipped off about an intruder earlier, but I doubt it. I would say they are half asleep, dreaming of baking-hot beaches and shimmering sand. They're burning up their last few moments and their dreams will stop here.

Without a sound, I take the gun and the hook, nestling one of them comfortably in the crook of each hand and crossing my hands over my chest. They have never seemed colder or heavier than they do now, as I break cover and emerge from the shadows. I stride towards the two men, approaching from behind, not giving them a chance. When I reach the first I freeze like a statue and wait. I am waiting for the lightning. It seems a long time coming. When the shadows are lit up and the lights disappear, I plant the hook in the first man's head. A clean, swift, sweeping movement which pierces his skull and releases his spirit. He slumps to my feet. I hold on to him like a great slab of meat to stop him collapsing altogether. The other man has turned towards me. He sees his colleague hanging limply in my hands, looks up at me and stares, transfixed with terror. I aim the gun at him and wait. I know he doesn't understand. Several seconds pass. As the thunder echoes round I bring him down with one bullet. He crumples without a sound. It's all too easy.

I don't know how many bodies I have hidden in the last few days, but it's a task that often seems to fall to me. It is the physical side of it that bothers me, because lifeless bodies are difficult to heave about. Luckily the dark hedges are just what I need. I lie the men down underneath one, but not before taking their handcuffs. The driving rain is washing the blood away at my feet, carrying it into the warmth of the earth.

Now I am standing facing the house. I head for the nearest end to look in at a large well-lit window. The maid is busy loading the dishwasher in a spotless kitchen with huge expanses of work surface and all the latest equipment. I watch her working. A little dear of about fifty: dark hair, black uniform, white apron, worn down by hard work and servitude. She seems to have finished for the evening, running the cloth over the sink and switching the machine on. Then she carefully seals a huge plastic bag swollen with the filthy excrescences of family life. Looking at the layout of the interior I see that the utility room has a door to the outside. I decide to weave my web there. A back door: now that's a useful way to put the rubbish out without disturbing the master of the house. I walk over to it and wait for her on the doorstep. She won't be long.

When she does appear, we come face to face. Everything happens so quickly. I just have time to glimpse my reflection in her eyes before they glaze over. There is precious little to get my teeth into in her spirit. I even suck up the scream she fails to produce. In the end she falls into my arms, limp and dead. Another body to shift. I drag her away and lean her against a tree trunk beneath the dark branches. Then I go back and finish taking the rubbish out for her. I leave the door ajar and walk round the outside of the house.

Further on I notice some French windows with the curtains

drawn. The lights are on inside. People are moving around. The curtains are edged with bear cubs and clowns. I move closer and watch the show through the narrow gap. There they are: the girls, sitting in their room, playing. I can see they are having fun. Two young children, the two little girls I came here for. No more than seven or eight, sitting on the floor in their pyjamas. They are the first children I have seen since coming back. They seem to be getting the most out of life. They have laid their tea-set out on the floor with great care, and now they are cutting up bits of Play-Doh to put on the plates as food. The triple glazing separates us, but I can hear their high-pitched voices. The younger of the two picks up a miniature saucepan and puts it carefully on to a cardboard box which I guess is the stove. From time to time one of them gets up and walks across the room, disappearing for a moment. Then I watch what the other one is doing and try, without success, to grasp what they are saying, probably trivial questions, laughter and predictable replies. On the off chance, I try the handle. All the doors seem to be locked and this one is no exception. My attempt creates a dull clunk in the mechanism. The little girls stop their game and spin round towards the sound. I disappear quickly and carry on with my reconnaissance.

At last I come to the bay window of the living room and there he is, with his shepherdess. It is a huge room furnished with valuable pieces and tasteful paintings. He is working at a magnificent desk with delicate marquetry work. She is lying on the sofa reading. They are younger than I expected, strong, in perfect health: his shoulders are as wide as her waist is narrow. So here he is then, the great master of impregnation, the man who took everything from me. Mind you, he's no oil painting, sitting in the glow of his laptop, which doesn't manage to wipe the tan off his face. I look away and finish my circuit round the building, which gives me an opportunity to see them from various angles through different windows. She is very pretty, blonde, her long hair coiled up in a chignon. He looks like a strong character, I can tell by the lines on his forehead, which furrow from time to time as he taps away at his keyboard, pausing when he comes to a problem.

I return to the back door, push it open and creep in silently. It feels hot and dry inside. The floor tiles are almost warm. I take off the leather coat, which is heavy with water, and let it drop to the floor. Now I am standing naked in the kitchen. I'm frightened. I don't really understand what I came here for any longer. I put the hook, handcuffs and gun down on the draining board. I only have one bullet left. That's plenty to kill four people. I open a few cupboards and pour myself a glass of water before tackling the horror that is to follow. In order to get on with it there is something I absolutely must have, and I can't find one in any of the countless drawers in this room. I look for a long time and start getting impatient and making too much noise. When I'm about to give up I finally find what I'm looking for: a set of knives in every size, attached to the white wall. I sigh, go over to them and choose. They are beautiful things. Some are long and narrow, others short and wide, substantial or delicate, in metal that ranges from gleaming blue to matt grey. I set my heart on a glorious specimen, one that is slightly smaller than the average, but exquisitely proportioned: it's going to be perfect for children.

I pick up the knife and walk out of the kitchen, through an

archway. To my left is the door to the sitting room. I'll have an opportunity to make my entrance there soon enough. To my right, a long corridor. From my reconnaissance work I deduce that the children's bedroom is down at the end, probably on the left. I start walking and come across an exotic pedestal table with a modern lamp on it. No doubt about it: the Ménards have good taste, and they have the funds, too. The laughing sounds closer. I stop outside the door, my hand on the cold brass handle. The two little girls are playing behind this panel of oak. Every now and then I hear their feet padding softly as they run up and down. Before I go in, I close my eyes and try to picture a suitable modus operandi. I will probably stab them in the chest, one after the other, to avoid too much screaming. It will stop them breathing and their lungs will fill with blood. What will their flesh feel like when I drive the blade in? Will I find the strength to do it? I force myself to imagine their deaths, as if watching a film. It makes me feel almost happy.

The corridor seems to be getting darker with every passing minute. I suddenly feel horribly giddy. Here I am coldly preparing myself to commit the unspeakable. What sort of spell did they cast over me, turning me into this heinous assassin, this thing with no reflection? I wait for the murderous rage I was promised. It will all be over for me soon. I will be leaving. I think of Hélène. She may well be waiting for me somewhere. For a moment I think I could turn back, back to her, but in the bottom of my heart I know I no longer have the strength. I came into her life and left again. It is time.

So I turn the handle, open the door, go in and close it behind me. There is no bed, so it is not, in fact, a bedroom, but a playroom. The younger of the two girls is sitting against the wall to the right of the door. She looks up at my penis, exposing her throat. Without a moment's hesitation I bury the knife in it and give a sharp tug to the side. She coughs, gurgles and falls over on to her back. There are red bubbles coming out of her mouth. I step over to the older girl, who is making an extraordinary high-pitched screaming sound. She hasn't stopped screaming for two hours now: no one's going to come. I stab her three times in the chest with all my strength. She collapses and sets about dying. It takes longer with the heart, but it's cleaner. In a way there's something more noble about it too. So I wait for the first one to stop spilling her blood and for the second to stop groaning. The knife feels sticky in my hand. The minutes go by. I wipe the blade on the curtains and enjoy the show. All this blood in among all these toys. It makes me feel strange, but I can't really define how. I give up trying and wait. They're still moving, it takes a while. When all movement has stopped, I busy myself doing what I came here for. I empty them out, praying that hell will take me this time.

I head back along the corridor. It felt long on the way, but now it seems to have no end. My God, what am I doing? I walk past the pedestal table and into the kitchen where I put the knife into the sink. I pick up the gun, which is no longer dripping with rainwater, and head for the sitting room. I open the door and go in. They don't see me. I suppose they must think I'm the maid, and, of course, neither of them would bother looking up at her. I cock the gun and Ménard says something at last.

'Ah, Maria, could you bring us some tea, please? A sliver of lemon for me and a drop of milk for Mrs Ménard. Quickly, come on.'

In reply I throw his daughter's head on to the keyboard of his laptop, splattering blood all over the desk, the wall and his clothes. The computer sputters and short-circuits. He screams, pushes his chair back and leaps to his feet.

'Jean, what's going on?' his wife asks, also jumping up. 'What's all that blood, for God's sake?'

The head has rolled on to the floor. She hasn't seen it. He has though. He can't take his eyes off it and just keeps saying, 'No, no.' His wife takes one step towards him and then she sees it, then she starts to wail as I've never heard anyone wail before. She makes a noise that sounds as if it never wants to die. So I feel obliged to accelerate the process.

'Oh, shut up!'

They turn towards me. She starts screaming again when she sees me. It's only then that I realise they hadn't noticed I was there, despite the stench that comes with me. Did they think this head just fell out of the sky for no reason? She won't stop screaming. I fire. He jumps out of his skin and she shuts up. He backs away. She brings her hands over her stomach, groans, totters and falls to her knees. At least I'll have some peace.

'Do you know what I am?' I ask, turning towards him.

I threaten him with my empty gun. I have just taken pleasure in killing someone, at last. In my other hand I am holding his daughter's intestines. He is riveted by them. Any normal man would hurl himself at me, gun or no gun, but not him. I now realise just how wrong Baron Saturday was: Ménard is not vital to the system.

He could not care less for his own safety, nothing can get to him unless it disrupts the whole organisation. He wants to survive, wants to carry on, so that he can perpetuate the present, creating an illusion of permanence. Of course, he knows exactly what he is dealing with, and he is very careful not to look me in the eye. His wife is gasping and moaning at his feet. She'll take a good while to die and I hope she doesn't miss one bit of her agony. Ménard won't answer or look at either of us, so I shake my hand at him.

'You see these, these are your daughter's guts. The little one's. I asked her her name, but she didn't have the strength to answer. Her innards are still warm, you know. You were just next door when I killed them, and you didn't hear a thing. Do you realise it was a while before they died? It's only in films that people die just like that, straight away. In real life it's much slower, especially for little bodies like that, so full of life. I watched them go out slowly like lights, they tried to call you all the way through, but you didn't come. How do you think they felt about you when they died?'

He doesn't say anything, he seems hypnotised by the dripping intestines. My temper flares. His wife is on her knees, still groaning. I don't know what she would do to me if she could. Whatever it is, she's trying to do it right now. Summoning all the strength of a mother's desperation, she pulls herself slowly to her feet, leaning on a luxurious armchair and daubing it abundantly with her blood. Her every movement is pathetically slow and her grimace of agony is painful to behold. She takes three steps towards the fireplace. Ménard still does not look at her as she picks up the poker. I laugh. For the first time in days I laugh properly, throwing my head back.

'Looks like she's got more fight in her than you,' I tell him. Then I turn to her and add: 'That's right, come on. Come and crack my head open with your little bit of metal.'

She staggers towards me, growling in fury. I am amazed at the sheer quantity of blood she has lost. Still she carries on towards me, one step at a time. She stumbles. I encourage her, just as I used to encourage my son when he was learning to walk. When she is barely two metres away, she tries to raise the heavy rod, but it slips from her hand and falls. She too crumples to the floor, sitting with her back against the wall, gasping for air. Then, slowly, she slides on to her side, coughing. She tries to grasp the poker, her fingers flailing in vain. Her eyes can probably no longer see.

'Is that it? What a pity, my love. I almost thought you'd manage it. You'll have to excuse me, I've got unfinished business with your old man now.'

Ménard makes up his mind to speak at last.

'You can't kill me. We gave you eternal life. You should be grateful to us.'

'How many lives did you sacrifice for this one, which isn't worth living?'

'Don't you think that's enough now? You've got to stop blindly destroying things, and make the most of this new life.'

'New life?' I ask bitterly. 'I had a life and you used it to get rid of the Bouteille girl.'

'I don't remember anything –'

'You took my wife, my children, my whole world,' I interrupt.

'You've just done the same to me.'

'Is that all the effect it has on you?'

He looks at his wife who seems to be quietly begging for help.

'What good is this going to do?' he asks. 'We can't put the clock back. That's why we'll never understand each other. You live in the present with nothing but hate, and all your dreams are in the past. We live and dream in the future.'

'You're the most abject, contemptible man I've ever met.'

'No. I'm a perfect cog in the system and I'm unfailingly happy.'

'Who's in charge?'

'Soon no one will be any more. The Governors came here to be safe from any kind of attack, but they disappeared too. Impregnation and maturation are gradually catching up with us and this estate is falling apart. It won't be long before nothing can be attributed to any one individual – that whole concept will be obsolete.'

'Don't you ever want to stop blindly obeying?' I ask.

'I don't intend to end up coming back like you.'

'What happened to all the children? I saw a school with no children. Where are they?'

He opens his mouth, but says nothing. He looks uncomfortable for the first time in our conversation. Perhaps he was not expecting the question. The silence goes on, and on. He seems to have decided not to answer. I am losing patience. Anger and rage wash over me in huge waves. I hurl the intestines into his face with a flick of my hand. They fall to the floor with a loud, wet sound.

'Where are the children?' I whisper.

Again there is silence, then he speaks at last, staring at the floor in front of him.

'They don't cope well with impregnation. It… kills them. It's to do with the doses, but also because their enzymes just aren't mature enough. We're working on it.'

'If that's the case, where did your daughters come from?'

'We got them by cloning their mother. A little privilege for the residents of this estate, shall we say. It's the price we have to pay for all the good things Ariel has given us.'

'Ariel?'

'Yes, Ariel, the angel, the bringer of light. That's what we called the mix when we finished perfecting it. We've been using it for nearly thirteen years now... in fact, I think you were one of the first we used it on "life size", so to speak. We were, and still are, very pleased with it.'

'What did you do to get me to take the stuff?'

'That's our little secret.'

'Don't play games with me.'

'With you it wasn't difficult. The procedure is set up using a third party. Wasn't there someone with you that evening?'

Of course there was. I have thought back to that last evening so many times I feel as if I can remember every face there. Yet there is one face I cannot see clearly: the other man's. I nod in silence.

'Well, there you are,' he says. 'It's not very complicated, you know: colourless, odourless, painless.'

'How can you give me these details when just now you said you didn't remember?'

'That's what impregnation does for you.'

'And what about the whole population? How do you drug so many people?'

'We used grains from the most widely used cereal crops. We had to use force on people who refused to cultivate them, and cunning on those who weren't sure about eating them. It was tricky, I admit. We had to work very hard. But that bit of African genetic wizardry was slightly beyond us, I'll give you that. Still, the results were more than in keeping with what we were expecting.'

'And what about maturation? You use mobile phones, don't you?'

'No. We use mirrors. Straightforward mirrors. If you only knew everything we know about the power of reflection.'

'You hadn't anticipated the secondary effects though, had you?'

'No. Well, not all of them.'

'Look at her,' I tell him, pointing at his wife on the floor. She is motionless now, except for her lips which are still moving, though not a word comes out. 'And look at me. Look at what your angel did, an angel that kills children and brings dead people back to life. Do you think my anger's going to stop at this? Who do you think this Ariel got his light from?'

He says nothing, seems incapable of emotion. I can tell he is thinking how to play this, and all the others are thinking with him. They know they can save him. They want him to maintain the integrity of the structure. For all my sermonizing, I am feeling seriously uncomfortable. Sooner or later I am going to have to stop preaching and start killing. I have no bullets left. The hook and the knife are in the kitchen, and he is carefully avoiding my eyes. If he chose to leap at me and break my neck, I am absolutely sure he would succeed. Another surge of anger is about to wash over me. I am not afraid of him. I am no more afraid of him than of the damnation to come. I am afraid of pain and moral decay, but I am no longer afraid of hell.

'You could just exist without causing all this evil,' he says, interrupting my thoughts.

'If that was going to work, your agents would have to stop hunting me down.'

'You have to agree you have a propensity for aggression. We have to protect ourselves, even if we don't get rid of you. The others like you are the same. In fact, you're like copies of each other, and we've often had run-ins with you. You must try to understand our point of view.'

'What about you? Have you made any attempt to understand us? All I've done is try to find answers to the questions which plagued me when I came back from the dead. I didn't do anyone any harm, but you were there forcing me to kill. All I was looking for was answers.'

'We're working towards a world with no questions,' he said blandly.

'I can't accept that sort of alienation – I'm free.'

'No. None of us are any more. Ariel has spread on the air, in the water, in pollen, meat, sperm, blood. Governments fought over the formula for it, then they used it and it wasn't long before they too disappeared in the new order they helped to create. Our old ideals won't mean anything any more. I'm not saying they were good or bad. I'm just saying they won't mean anything, that's all. With Ariel the whole human race has embarked on a new evolutionary path. A high-performance machine, working at optimum output, limiting individual chaos to create a sublime whole. Just one thought for everyone: the thought of everyone.'

'And what about me?'

'Look at yourself,' he says contemptuously. 'You don't belong here. You can choose to stay and to live, but you'll never belong.'

'Why?'

'Because impregnation doesn't have any effect on you. You'll just carry on wandering around through a world you don't understand, and which doesn't accept you.'

'Let's see if you cope any better than me in this world then — have this,' I say throwing the gun on to the armchair behind him.

It lands with a soft, muffled thud. Startled, Ménard looks up and catches my eye for a moment. He looks away almost immediately. Everything happens very quickly after that. He spins round and lunges at the gun, which does not surprise me. Everything he said is just hot air. I throw myself after him, lowering myself to the ground on the way and picking up the poker. He doesn't see me do it, but he can sense me just behind him. He grabs the gun, turns round and points it at me. He fires, just as I am preparing to strike, holding the poker firmly in both hands. He must be very surprised to hear a simple 'click', when he was hoping for an explosion — and that is the last of his emotions for the evening. He has very little time to express this astonishment, which I imagine rather than witness. I hit him across the temple with all the strength of my accumulated rage. It is a heavy blow, making a dull cracking sound. Things moved around inside. He falls on to his oriental carpet, the gun slips from his hand and under the sideboard. He stays on the ground, racked with convulsions. I hit him again and again, as I must have hit Agnès Bouteille, until the skull is so broken it has turned to pulp. I am still hitting him long after he has stopped moving, thinking about my wife and children.

I sit on the sofa for a long time. I am under no illusions about what will happen next. The Ménard lying at my feet in a pool of blood will soon be replaced by another who will be at least as efficient. Tomorrow, no one will even remember him, but everything Ménard helped to create will carry on, indifferent to the men that are part of it. They will find some way of getting by without children, or they will make them out of thin air, and the ordered world will be perpetuated. I would rather all this happened without me. I would like to see Lucy again. So I sit there quite motionless and at peace, as the little red lights glide over the floor and walls, and converge on my head. Curtain.

I am walking along a gloomy grey-pebbled shore, following the line of the water, though I do not know why. Perhaps this is the morning after a night of thick mists. Perhaps it is the evening of a sunless day. The fog seems to have settled in for ever, covering everything in impenetrable silence. A wooden pontoon slowly appears in front of me, raised on spindly posts. I climb on to it and walk along above the lifeless water, a black mirror in this wan greyness. My footsteps make no sound. Noise, light and movement have never reached this place. There is a heavy boat moored at the very end. A man is sitting in it with a long pole in his hand. He is wearing a thick robe of gleaming black fur. His face is hidden by a hood. I stop above him and speak. I can hear my voice, even though no sound reaches my ears.

'You said you would come back to take me over, didn't you?'

The man does not answer. I do not need him to. I look at the boat, then at the man, and try in vain to see the far shore. A few minutes pass. I speak to him again.

'Where are you taking me?'

I am waiting for an answer that never comes. I give up. I am alone. A quick glance around and I get into the boat. It sways, but the water shows not the slightest ripple. I sit down and he stands up and pushes on the pole. The pontoon slips away, until it is swallowed up in the fog. Then only the black of the water and the grey of the air are left. It is then that I see the first particles of ash landing on my hand. I look up. They are emerging from the air and landing slowly, perfectly straight now that there is no wind to waft them. Lucy will not be on the far bank.